Drawn by E. Jappe, age 86
23 July, 1975, Stage Two, time-confused

i

Available from the Publsher:

Edward Feil Productions
4614 Prospect Avenue
Cleveland, Ohio 44103

Revised: 1992

Dutch Translation: 1989

German Translation: 1990

French Translation: 1991

Library of Congress Catalog Number: 89-184004
ISBN#: 1-878169-00-9

V/F

VALIDATION®

The Feil Method

How To Help Disoriented Old-Old

by

Naomi Feil, ACSW

Revised with Vicki de Klerk-Rubin

To Ed Feil whose films are
worth a million words.

With grateful acknowledgment to
Piet de Klerk for his insight and expertise
in the revision of this book

PREFACE

Here's to a wise old age!

This book is for all those who care for and about disoriented old-old people.
Validation helps helpers become comfortable with disoriented old-old who freely express feelings.
Validation accepts people as they are.
Validation tells the reason behind the feelings.
Validation helps the disoriented old-old reach *their* goals - not ours.

BIOGRAPHY

Naomi Feil grew up in the Montefiore Home for the Aged in Cleveland, Ohio, where her professional parents pioneered rehabilitation. Mrs. Feil received her Master's Degree in 1956 at Columbia University, New York School of Social Work, specializing in group work with the aged. She directed Group Work Services at Bird S. Coler Hospital on Welfare Island and W. Hodson Community Center, both in New York. In 1963, she returned to Montefiore Home to continue her father's 1947 research and practice with disoriented old-old residents. Naomi Feil developed Validation between 1963 and 1980, as a group worker at Montefiore Home and as an Adjunct Instructor at the School of Applied Social Sciences, Case Western Reserve University, Cleveland, Ohio. She now practices Validation with residents at day care centers, veterans administration hospitals, and as a consultant to nursing homes and families. She also leads workshops throughout Europe, Australia and North America.

Mrs. Feil is a member of the Academy of Certified Social Workers (ACSW) and is listed in "Outstanding Professionals in Human Services," "Who's Who of American Women," and "The World Who's Who of Women." In addition to *V/F Validation*®*: The Feil Method*, she has published material on aging in gerontological journals, books, magazines, and the "Guide to Inter-Generational Programming" for the National Council on Aging. Mrs. Feil has also written nine award-winning film scripts on aging for Edward Feil Productions. A former actress in Off-Broadway theater, she uses her performing skills to teach empathy with the disoriented old-old.

TABLE OF CONTENTS

PART ONE: WHAT IS VALIDATION?

PART TWO: THE FOUR STAGES OF DISORIENTATION

PART THREE: IMPLEMENTING INDIVIDUAL VALIDATION

PART ONE

WHAT IS VALIDATION ?

The Beginning

In 1963, after seven years of working with oriented, healthy elderly in community centers, I began working with old-old people that is, people over the age of 80, who were disoriented, at the Montefiore Home for the Aged in Cleveland, Ohio.[1] My initial goals were to help severely disoriented old-old to face reality and relate to each other in a group. In 1966, I concluded that helping them to face reality is unrealistic. Each person was trapped in a world of fantasy.[2] Exploring feelings and reminiscing encouraged group members to respond to each other. Music stimulated group cohesion and feelings of well-being. I abandoned the goal of reality orientation when I found group members withdrew, or became increasingly hostile whenever I tried to orient them to an intolerable present reality.

One very disoriented old-old woman used to sing, "Daisy, Daisy, I'm half crazy...", and then explained the reason for her "dementia", "It's better when you're crazy. Then it doesn't matter what you do."

Another disoriented group member rose to leave the room, saying, "I have to go home now to feed my children." I said, "Mrs. Kessler, you can't go home. Your children are not there. You now live in a home for older people, the Montefiore Home." She answered, "I know that. Don't be stupid! That's why I have to leave this place. Right now. I have to go to my own home to feed my children!" No amount of presentation of present reality could convince Mrs. Kessler. She felt useless in a nursing home. She wanted her own home and her old role as mother of her three children to feel useful. She withdrew from me, muttering to herself, "What does she (pointing to me) know. Who does she think she is!"

Mr. Rose accused the administrator of castrating him in the attic. I tried to orient Mr. Rose to reality for five years. When the administrator retired, Mr. Rose said to me, "You're right. He didn't hurt me. I'm no good. I never was."

Those were the last words he spoke to me. He dropped his cane and never walked again. On the arm of his wheelchair he walked with his fingers, muttering, "Buckeye and 105th," over and over again. Buckeye and 105th was the corner where his law office had been located. He repeatedly pounded his left knee, which hurt him because of Paget's Disease saying, "Damn Judge...Damn Judge...Damn Judge..." His father had told him years ago, "You'll never amount to anything. You're no good." His sister told me he never accomplished much. Like a good boy, he bottled up his rage, hurt and guilt. He listened to his father. His father had castrated him with words.

Now, in his old-old age, all alone in his wheelchair, he struggled to resolve his rage and guilt. I never listened when he blamed father figures for hurting him. He wanted me to validate his rage. He blamed the judge, the administrator, the doctors, God (his father figures), for ruining his life. His father had punished him in the attic. He returned to the past to tell his father how he felt; to re-store his father's love; to justify himself in this world. Nobody validated him. He struggled alone. His body movements grew feeble. Slowly he lost his purpose for living, and vegetated until death. He moved from Stage One, malorientation, to Stage Four, vegetation, invalidated.[3]

Mr. Rose and hundreds like him taught me to abandon reality orientation with these disoriented old-old. I learned Validation from the people with whom I worked. I learned that they have the wisdom to survive by returning to the past.

Basic Beliefs

To validate is to acknowledge the feelings of a person. To validate is to say that their feelings are true. Denying feelings invalidates the individual. Validation uses empathy to tune into the inner reality of the disoriented old-old. Empathy, or walking in the shoes of the other, builds trust. Trust brings safety. Safety brings strength. Strength renews feelings of worth. Worth reduces stress. With empathy, the Validation worker picks up their clues and helps put their feelings into words. This validates them and restores dignity.

Some disoriented old-old no longer need to return to the past when they feel strong, loved and worthwhile in the present time. Others choose to remain in the past. There is no single or simple formula for everyone. All feel happier when validated.[4]

Validation is:

- a developmental theory for old-old mal- and disoriented people;
- a method for categorizing their behavior;
- specific techniques to help mal- and disoriented very old people regain dignity both through individual Validation and through Validation groups.

Validation Goals:

- restore self-worth
- reduce stress
- justify living
- work towards resolving unfinished conflicts from the past
- reduce the need for chemical and physical restraints
- increase verbal and non-verbal communication
- prevent withdrawal inward to Vegetation
- improve gait and physical well-being

Theoretical Assumptions

Basic principles developed by behavioral, analytical and humanistic psychologies underlie the theoretical assumptions in Validation:

A. Accept your client without judgement. (Carl Rogers)
B. The therapist cannot give insight or change behavior if the client is not ready to change *or does not have the cognitive capacity for insight*. (Sigmund Freud)
C. Know your client as a unique individual. (Abraham Maslow)
D. Feelings that are expressed, and then acknowledged and validated by a trusted listener, will become less intense. When ignored or denied, feelings gain strength. "The cat

ignored, becomes the tiger." (Carl Jung)

E. Each stage of life has a unique task that we must face at a prescribed time in the human life span. We must struggle to accomplish the task, then move on to the next task. (Erik Erikson)

F. An ignored task demands to be heard at a later stage. (Erik Erikson)

G. Human beings struggle for balance (homeostasis). (S. Zuckerman)

H. When recent memory (short term memory) fails, very old humans restore balance by retrieving early memories. When eyesight fails, they use the mind's eye to see. When hearing goes, they listen to sounds from the past. (Wilder Penfield)

I. Early, well-established memories survive to very old age. (F.G. Schettler and G.S. Boyd)

J. The brain is not the exclusive regulator of behavior in very old age. Behavior is a combination of physical, social, and intrapsychic changes that happen during the life span. (Adrian Verwoerdt)

K. Autopsies have shown that many very old persons survive significant brain damage and stay relatively oriented. (Charles Wells)

L. There is a reason behind the behavior of disoriented very old people. (Naomi Feil)

M. Each human being is valuable - no matter how disoriented. (Naomi Feil)

Erik Erikson's Theory of Life Stages and Tasks[5]

Erik Erikson, the famous psychologist created a theory of Developmental Life Stages and Life Tasks, that are based upon the interrelationship of our biological, mental, and social capacities and drives. These change as we age. Success in accomplishing a task at a certain age depends on how well we have accomplished the earlier task at an earlier age. We are always struggling to accomplish our tasks from birth to death.

Stage	Task	Failure to achieve task
1. Infancy	Learn to trust	Distrust, I'm unlovable
2. Childhood	Learn to follow rules, control	Shame, guilt, blame
3. Adolescence	Find own identity; separate from parents	Insecurity, role-diffusion; I'm nobody unless somebody loves me.
4. Adult	Learn to be intimate; be responsible for feelings, failures and successes	Isolation, dependency
5. Mid-Years	Generate new activities when old roles wear out	Stagnation; holding on to outworn roles
6. Old Age	Tie up living; find inner strength, integrity	Despair; I might as well be dead

The infant, warm and snuggled against mother's breast, is put down abruptly when the phone rings. Now the infant is cold, hungry, frightened and angry. In infancy we must learn to trust that mother will come back. We will survive the cold, hunger pangs, fury, and fear. Mother proves to us again and again that we are loveable. We can live through hard times. She loves us. We can love ourselves, because we are loveable.

But if the infant cannot be sure that mother will return, it never learns to trust and enters childhood loaded with distrust. In kindergarten the child runs, stumbles, falls and accuses the nearest classmate, "You tripped me on purpose!" As an infant he couldn't count on mother's love, never learned that he was loveable. As a child, he does not love himself and cannot trust himself. Now he is the victim, hunting for a destroyer. He denies responsibility for bad things that happen. This child becomes a blamer. Instead of trusting that they can survive, blamers suspect society of doing them in. When this child becomes an old man who falls because his arthritic knees will no longer hold him, he will blame the cleaning woman for deliberately waxing the floor to make him fall. When this old man's eyes blur, he will blame the maintenance man for putting in defective light bulbs.

Fears that were never faced in childhood reappear in disguise in old age. Present-day fears trigger memories of early fears. The little girl who was locked in a dark closet for a terrified moment by an older brother becomes the old woman who shrieks when her eyes fail, or when she is alone in the dark. A physical loss in old age triggers a memory of an earlier feeling of loss. Similar feelings attract each other like a magnet. They fly through time.

In childhood we learn control. We follow rules. We learn that we can make mistakes and still control our world. If we miss the potty once or twice, we are still loved. We are proud when we become toilet trained. "Look! I did the right thing at the right time in the right place." We fall off our bike the first twenty times we try to ride it. Still, we try again. The infant who learned to trust becomes the child who can risk riding "no-hands". The child may fall, but will not fall apart.

But if our parents repeat over and over, "Never mess up!"; if we learn that love needs perfection, never soiling, never spilling, never falling, never crying, never forgetting, and so on..., we add another load to our backpack. We carry with us to old age the urgent need to keep tight control. Never expose feelings. Can't afford a slip up. If we want to be loved, we must pay the price. We keep our fingers wrapped tight around the handlebars to avoid falling off our bikes and do not risk making mistakes. In old age when we can't help making mistakes, when controls loosen, we become the hoarders. We gather our possessions, putting the right things in the right places. The old man who fears losing his virility, gathers his canes, knives, keys, and wallet. If he forgets or loses things, he blames his children, neighbors, or the nursing home staff for stealing his possessions. He has never faced the losses that come with old age. He has never learned to trust himself to live through hard times. The old woman who always needs to be in control and who is now incontinent, shouts with fury, "There is a leak in my ceiling. Every time it rains, it drips on my bed. Nobody will fix it." Nobody can fix the losses of aging. This old woman blames everyone else for her deficiencies. She is afraid of making mistakes; then nobody will love her. She hoards objects in her purse: pens to reassure her that she will never lose her perfect handwriting; pins and needles, papers, tissues, napkins, food, to guard herself against hard times and keep herself together. The more she loses control over her world, the more she hoards her things.

As teenagers, our task is to cut the cord, to rebel. When you are 15, mother can turn into a wicked witch and father a dreadful dragon breathing the fire of hated authority. We reject their rules, defy them. We must discover our own values, make up our own rules. We fight to find out who we are; to separate from our loved ones. We've learned in infancy, that our parents love us even when we fight them. We can risk rebellion.

But, if we do not have and hold unconditional love from our parents, rebellion is risky. If we fight and disobey, mother and father might not love us any more. They might abandon us. We will be alone. Therefore, we capitulate, are good, always do what mommy and daddy want. We never learn who we are - ourselves, separate from our parents, separate from authority. We are the teacher's good student, the boss' good worker. We borrow our identity from the outside world, never having found our own. We never cut the cord. We never learn to "be," without our family, without home, without our legs, in our wheelchairs, all alone. We always have to be somebody's something. This type of old woman clings to her children, to her neighbors, to the nursing home staff. She becomes the martyr; complains about her aches and pains, giving the world her "organ recital", "My head hurts, my stomach hurts, my back aches," and so on. She whines, "One mother can raise ten children, but ten children can't take care of one mother."

In adulthood our task is to get close to another human being. If as a teenager we gained a sense of identity, we can afford to say, "I love you," or, "I hate you," without fear of rejection. Our ability to love is not dependent on being loved. If we are rejected, we will survive. We have our own identity, separate from the loved one. We can risk being hurt. But, if we fail to accomplish our earlier life tasks, we will not reach out for intimacy. If we could never trust ourselves to take our hands off the handlebars as children, how can we trust ourselves to survive the inner bumps of adulthood? Haunted by the terror of abandonment in infancy; the agonizing embarrassment of failure as a child; the fear of rejection as a teenager; we stay apart from others. We become isolated and acquire a new load to carry into old age. We become a recluse. In the nursing home we sit alone. Without stimulation from the outside world, with failing eyesight and hearing, we retreat inward more and more.

Our fifth life task, in middle age, is to roll with the punches. We watch our wrinkles deepen, our hair thin. Our wrinkly skin doesn't fit the bones, the bags under our eyes won't unpack. We look in the mirror. Everything seems the same as it did five years ago, but it's all a little lower. Some of us suffer an onslaught, an avalanche of losses. We lose a spouse, a breast, a kidney, a job... and on and on. We face our losses. We grieve. We look in the mirror and accept the fact that we are aging and will not live forever. In middle age we move on; expand our repertoire for living; add new keys to the piano of our lives. A wife dies; a close friend is found. A job goes; we become a volunteer.

But, if we have learned that we must be perfect, that we cannot lose control, then we cannot spill our gut feelings, our grief to anyone. So, how can we face the wounds of middle age? Without our spouse, we are nobody. Without our job, we are nothing. Without our breasts, we are sexless. To survive, we deny the impact of our losses. We cannot risk learning new keys, so continue banging the same old key. We hang onto outworn roles. A widower rejects a new relationship - nobody is good enough. A music-lover refuses to buy a hearing aid - it's too expensive. An executive ridicules a volunteer job - his time is worth money. We are stuck clinging to outworn behaviors. In the third stage of disorientation (time confusion) a wheelchair becomes a filing cabinet so the executive can continue working; a hand becomes a baby for the woman who must remain a mother. A medicine cart is a tractor for the farmer who needs to plow his field. These very old people must hold onto their jobs. They have nothing else to do. They are locked in because they have only one key.

Erikson says that the final life task is to review life. It's time to look backward, to sort out what we were. We review the past in order to preview the future. One woman says, "What was I? I was a mother and I made a lot of mistakes, but I learned from my mistakes. I did a lot of good things too." We figure out where we are. Another chimes in, "I am now an old woman. My husband is gone. But, I can share feelings with close friends." We think about what we could have been. A third declares, "I wish I had been a great actress, but I wasn't. Instead, I used my acting skills to become a good teacher. I like myself. Despite my unfulfilled dreams, my mistakes, despite my losses, I am glad I was born. I respect myself. I have integrity. I can compromise. I can accept what I am, what I was and what I wasn't. I like me. Life is worth living. Although I'm in a wheelchair, I am pulling my act together." Those old-old have faced their tasks along the way, and now they deliberately reminisce, accepting the choices they have made, accepting themselves as they are.

Integrity in old age is recognizing one's strengths in spite of weakness. "Integrity is the merger between the actual self and the idealized self" according to Erikson.[6] With integrity, the old person counts on deep self-respect to heal the inevitable bruises that come with age. With integrity, I can risk a new life style when old patterns no longer work.

But, if you can't trust anyone to love you when you begin to lose your physical energy; when your eyes blur, your hair thins, your recent memory wavers, you are retired...then life is a mud puddle and you're stuck in it. You may think, "Nobody cares if I live or die. I wish I were dead." Without deep self-acceptance to outweigh failure, there is despair.

Despair, if ignored, rumbles and turns into depression. Depression is an internal temper tantrum. Rage, rebellion, shame, guilt, love... emotions that have been successfully bottled up for a lifetime, gain strength while locked inside. Bearing a backpack that becomes unbearable, we move towards old-old age. Humans are living longer and longer. The old-old have become a new breed of people. Pneumonia is no longer "the old person's cure at age 65." Statistics show that most of us will reach very old age.

Each stage of life has its own unique task. Ignore it, and the task makes a second entrance in a later stage. We get second and third chances to accomplish our life tasks. We seldom accomplish a life task the first time around. And no life task is completely finished. You should keep facing your feelings, being honest with yourself throughout life.[7] If, at 62, you fail to find a street in a strange town, and begin to blame the faulty street signs, you can face the fact that you are a blamer. You can express fear of becoming blind to a close friend. You can search for alternative ways of seeing. If you shy away from friendships, face your fear of intimacy, the pangs of rejection. You can change and not stay stuck in old patterns of behavior. Human beings with billions of brain cells, can regroup and add new connections. Our brains are "plastic." Heat plastic and it changes its shape.

We are struggling throughout life.[8] Seldom is any life task completely accomplished before the next one appears on the scene. We always need to go back to pick up the stray pieces. The unfinished task nags and follows us to very old age. If we continue to deny its existence, if we refuse to face it, the task waits until our controls weaken. We forget our entrance cues. We forget our lines. We have waited too long, it is too late. We lose the desire and the ability to change. Insight, the intellectual grasp of feelings, the "AHA!" is hard enough to achieve when we are physically intact. Facing feelings makes us vulnerable. Facing feelings is scary. We lose balance. In old age, each day brings another physical loss. At 83, we will not risk a heart attack by facing bottled-up feelings that terrify us. If we have ignored our important feelings, they finally flaunt us in our old age, when we have lost our controls and we are at the mercy of our care-givers. Buried for a lifetime, feelings finally erupt.

Feil's Resolution versus Vegetation Stage:
The Stage Beyond Integrity

Stage	Task	Failure to achieve task
7. Old-old age	Resolving of the past	Vegetation

In 1963, when I returned to work in the nursing home where I grew up, I found that most of the 170 residents were oriented, integrated human beings who had learned to compromise. They rolled with the punches of old age and still enjoyed living, despite physical and intellectual deficiencies. Only 23 residents had become confused or disoriented. Their ages ranged from 80 to 101 years. Nobody wanted them. They were the blamers, the martyrs, moaners, wanderers, yellers, pacers and the pounders. I didn't know it then, but each one had accumulated, during more than seven decades, a backpack of festering feelings. These were the very old people with whom I worked in the Special Service Wing, separated from the oriented residents who resented their "crazy" behaviors. Staff, too, wanted little to do with those very old people who could not or would not control their feelings and conform to society's expectations. In the 1960s, those 23 people would have died of pneumonia or heart disease, but modern medicine kept them alive. They had outlived their bodies.

These very old people gradually taught me that there is yet another task to accomplish in old-old age. I call this final task, the one beyond integrity, Resolution versus Vegetation. Very old people who are stuck with deep unresolved feelings left over from earlier life stages, often return to the past to resolve those feelings. They pack for their final move. They sort out dirty linen stashed in the storehouse of the past. They are busy, irresistibly drawn to wrap up loose ends. This is not a conscious move to the past, like Erikson's sixth and final stage. It is a deep human need: to die in peace. Those who achieve integrity in very old age never enter the Resolution stage. But, as humans continue to live longer, there will be a growing number of very old people who fall into the final Resolution stage. They need someone to listen, to validate their feelings. If no one listens, they withdraw to Vegetation. With no stimulation from the outside world, they become one of the living dead in our nursing homes. The Validation worker listens, knowing that there will never be a complete resolution, it is too late for insight. Feelings spill, unresolved until death. However, as the various feelings are acknowledged and validated, they dissipate. The old-old continue resolving, always preparing to die in a clean house.

The Reasons for Disorientation:
Denial of Physical and Social Losses

Physical Losses[9]

Physical aging means a gradual loss of useful tissue throughout the body. Human life span ranges to 120 years. People who hold onto outworn youthful roles deny normal signs of aging. Denial begins in middle age when wrinkles appear, skin fits loosely over shrinking bones, hair thins, night driving becomes difficult and some may develop breast tumors, prostate problems, cataracts, have small strokes and heart trouble. Fatty tissue accumulates. Brain and heart work harder. People who have no repertoire for facing losses are stuck. Aging will not stop. Denial of these physical, small "deaths" in middle and old age often leads to a final retreat into fantasy in old-old age.[10] In fact, physical deterioration helps the very old person who has unfinished life tasks, to accomplish the final task: restore the past in order to resolve it.

Loss of hearing causes some people to listen with their inner ear. The little boy who was constantly ridiculed in kindergarten because he could not control his urine, becomes the deaf old man who hears with his mind's ear. Instead of hearing his friend's playful, "You wanna bet?" the old man hears, "You're wet." The embarrassment of losing his hearing as an adult is like a magnet. It attracts the same feeling of shame he had as a boy when he wet his pants and the children taunted: "Sammy is wet! Sammy is wet!" The old Sam shakes his fist and walks away. He has lost his only friend. Loss of hearing awakens insecurities from the past. The only self-defense is denial for those who cannot face failures. Unsure, they begin to suspect others of ridiculing them. They retreat inward more and more. The former friend calls Sam "paranoid." It becomes easy to hear sounds from the past when the outside world is muffled. To ease his suffering, the old man hears his mother's voice.

If, as an adult, he had worked through that feeling of shame about wetting his pants, he might have accepted his hearing loss as an old man and would not have withdrawn. He would not have the need to resolve unfinished feelings as an old man. Had he struggled with that life task at an earlier stage, he would not have to enter the Resolution stage of life.

Eyes change. When the outside world blurs, the inside world can clear up. In old age, the optic nerve suffers damage, the lens yellows. An old person with a damaged retina can use the mind's eye to see. Vivid (eidetic) images restore loved ones from the past. Schettler and Boyd wrote: "The earlier an image has been imprinted on memory, the longer it is retained."[11] Wilder Penfield found: "The patient, himself, can activate the memory from within..., without the use of the sense organs."[12] Streaks, created by the sun's reflections, become a fence for an 88 year woman whose Daddy warned her to keep the horses inside the fence. Strapped in her chair, seeing with her vivid inner sight, hearing her father's voice with her mind's ear, smelling the past, she shouts: "Daddy, the horses won't listen. They got out! I didn't mean it. Dad! Help!" This old woman resurrects her father to make peace. She is resolving old feelings of guilt. Her family could not afford to lose those horses. In a poetic and creative way she changes present to past time in her final life struggle to regain her father's approval.

The brain changes as we age. There is less glucose and oxygen for brain metabolism. The kinesthetic nervous system is damaged. The old-old person begins to lose control over muscles and glands. Bowel and bladder functions become difficult. The human brain has billions of nerve cells. In our 20s we lose a few thousand. By age 90, some people have suffered considerable damage to the brain. We all age differently, depending upon genetics and environment. Little strokes and damaged nerve cells (plaques and tangles in the brain) can cause recent memory loss. Some very old people lose the ability to think intellectually - to put similar things into categories. When our brains are complete we can easily put chairs, tables and desks into the category of "furniture." We can pass this intelligence test: "A chair is to a table as an apple is to ..." The very old person with damaged logical thinking cannot supply a word like "orange" or "banana." They can no longer think cognitively. They can no longer put minutes, hours, days, weeks, months, years, into chronological order. The very old person is governed by memories. The keep track of their lifetime instead of minutes. Present and past blend. Clock time has gone. An old woman who cannot give up her only reason for living, motherhood, shouts, "I want to feed my children. They are hungry." She is told, "You just ate your breakfast. Your children are grown up." She yells louder, has forgotten that she just ate, doesn't want to eat in this sterile institution. This old woman doesn't remember that her children are grown up. She wants to feed them "rocky eggs and fish sticks."

Our kinesthetic nervous system can suffer damage. Sensory cells located throughout the body no longer inform the brain of the body's position. There is a blurring of the sense of self.[13] Dr. Smith no longer recognizes himself in the mirror when he is being shaved. He moves "beside himself." His brain no longer informs him of where he is or who he is. Dr. Smith had controlled his sexual instincts throughout his life. Now, they are finding the light of day. With a wicked gleam and a snicker of glee, he pats the breasts of the nursing assistant who is shaving him. When I asked, "Dr. Smith, do you know that you are making Sally feel uncomfortable?" he shooed me away, saying, "I am not Dr. Smith. Dr. Smith is in his office, practicing medicine. Now leave me alone. I'm busy." With damaged kinesthetic awareness, he uses his mind's eye to see Dr. Smith safely working in his laboratory or practicing medicine, the way he did for decades. Meanwhile, the man who is being shaved is busy working on completing his unresolved sexual feelings before death.

When the brain no longer knows where the body is in present reality, movements can take very old people back to work. If it is imprinted early on and reinforced through the years, our muscle memory stays. A slight flick of the wrist can take an old man back to his job as a carpenter. Motions can trigger e-motions. Mrs. Kulp, almost blind, holds her hand to her lips, caressing it, crooning and rocking her "hand baby." Here movements trigger visualizations. Her hand, soft like her baby, becomes her baby, and restores her identity as a mother.

Mr. Rose, a former lawyer, pounds his left knee that hurts him due to Paget's Disease. He shouts, "Damn judge, damn judge," eyes focused on his painful knee. His fingers travel up and down the arm of his wheelchair. They are his "feet", marching up and down, never stopping their motion, traveling back to the street where he practiced law. His knee hurts the way the judge hurt Mr. Rose when he lost his one big law case. Now, at 86, Mr. Rose punishes the judge and reviews his case, using familiar motions to restore the past. He is cleaning house before he dies. Patting, crooning, rocking, folding, tongue flicking, stroking, pounding, are physical movements that have a unique meaning to each disoriented very old person. They use familiar body movements to relive the past.

Social Losses

Death of loved ones, loss of one's job, loss of one's role as a worker, a mother, a child, or a friend, deprive old-old people of social stimulation. Touching, eye contact, recognition, validation from loved ones are basic human needs.[14] With little or no stimulation from the outside world people vegetate or die. Loss of stimulation leads to loss of identity. From infancy to old-old age, we need to interact with others. Stuck in their wheelchairs, some old-old lose touch with the outside world. Without feedback from other people, the old person can no longer match inner perceptions with what is actually happening outside.

Some very old people have always denied social losses. When a loved one died, they repressed the pain. Awareness of that pain would have created intolerable anxiety, caused panic, a flushed face, clammy hands, crying, sweating, inability to move, and increased their heartbeat. Pain can cause too much turmoil for a very old person to bear. They move inside themselves to survive the stress of facing unbearable reality all alone.

The Wisdom in Disorientation

The outside world blurs. What happens outside no longer matters. There is no one out there who cares. No one to love. Nothing to do. Physical deterioration of vision, hearing, reflective self-awareness and mobility contribute to the inward march. The old-old person no longer expends the energy to remember names of people in the present. Recent memory fades.

Alone in an apartment or trapped in a geriatric chair, they return to the time when they were somebody. They use their vivid memories to restore the past, when they were useful, productive, loved. They go back to a time when what they thought and did really counted. They relive the past to restore their dignity. They no longer care about pleasing people now. They get no satisfaction from present day reality. Human beings need stimulation in order to survive. The old-old stimulate themselves through memory. The past replaces the present. Night-time and daytime blend and overlap with no place to go, nothing to do, and no one to see at any time.

The early way of perceiving the world returns. They go back to the past searching for identity, meaning, to tie up living. The old-old express three basic human needs: 1. to be safe and loved; 2. to be useful and productive; 3. to express raw emotions. But, they no longer express these needs to people in the "here and now." Their communication is with people and objects from their past. They become egocentric, shutting out external reality. Speech centers deteriorate from disuse and from organic damage. They can no longer retrieve dictionary words, no longer define people or objects or relationships. They can no longer put "mother" into a category of "someone who has children." They return to well-established memories of their own mother. Brain circuits dormant since youth wake up and return to full consciousness. The old woman rocks to bring back her mother. The motion brings e-motion. She feels loved. Damage to rational thinking "frees and allows for greater non-verbal expression."[15] [16] When logical, learned speech goes, they return to "primal linguistic patterns."[17] This is not a second childhood. Well- learned memories persist throughout a lifetime. Wilder Penfield found that a stimulation in the present can play back an early memory with complete clarity. We can relive significant sights, sounds, smells and emotions that have been stored in our brain circuits since birth.[18]

When speech goes, very old disoriented people communicate with movements learned early in life. Their movements replace speech. The Swiss psychologist Piaget found that movements precede speech.[19] When an infant wants his absent mother, he learns to mimic her movements to bring her to mind. She rocked him. In imitating mother's rocking motion, he feels her presence. The rocking motion becomes the mother. At six months, the infant learned to imitate the sucking movements involved in nursing to remind himself of his mother. By moving his tongue and lips together, he has found his mother and is comforted. In school, when the structures in the brain are completely formed, the child learns to define the word "mother." He begins to understand how to classify.

A mother belongs in a category of anyone who has offspring. A puppy can have a mother, too. The word "mother" is classified and stored in the left brain. The child learns to think in the abstract, using dictionary words instead of made-up words to replace the actual objects. The sucking movement is stored in his permanent memory and forgotten intellectually. The child becomes a social animal.

In very old age, the disoriented person having lost those dictionary words, returns once more to well established, permanently stored movements. They move their lips to combine similar sounds and begin to rhyme as the sounds blend with one another. Like a finger painter, they smear vowels and consonants together that feel good, harmonize and are pleasurable to the tongue, teeth and lips. Childhood phrases, poems, prayers and songs return to very old people who cannot speak.

Further deterioration to intellectual functions also brings an increase in unique personal words which are a passage to the past. Early memories return to vivid consciousness. Mrs. Gogolick, peering at a curtain in the nursing home, says: *"That's symofile contabulation in the Fendall company!"* I discovered the meaning behind her unique word formations after ten years and much consultation with a linguist. My name is "Feil". Mrs. Gogolick was a file clerk. The curtain in my "Feil" company in the present was similar to the curtain in her "file clerk" office of the past. She smeared these sounds together to create her unique word: "symofile." Mrs. Gogolick had been a bookkeeper, added up figures, tabulated. She "figured out" or "tabulated" her observation about the curtain and created a new word, "contabulation." Her word doodle, "Fendall," is a combination of the phrase: "Memorable friends from the past." Mrs. Gogolick communicates by using her personal vocabulary.

Disoriented very old people move through the past resolving unfinished relationships. They express their uncontrollable feelings through movements and unique word formations.

Disorientation is regression, but the old person is not a child. The child can change and grow, wants to learn new facts, new words, can play games using established adult rules. The child is capable of cognitive reasoning, can learn to classify people and objects, wants to compare things that are alike and things that are different. The child learns to tell clock time, becomes aware of schooltime, playtime, and bedtime. It also learns to be self-aware and aware of others, can learn to control feelings and listen to the adult. Care-givers must teach children, give them roots, help them grow.

Disoriented old-old people have already rooted and grown. With the wisdom of crystallized human experience and intuition, they return to the past to clean house and to meet their basic human needs for love and identity. No longer willing to conform to society's rules, they review their earlier experiences according to their own rules. Returning to the past enables them to avoid the painful present, their feelings of uselessness and aloneness. They will not be aware of the present: day, time or place. Why keep track of chronological time when there is no place in it for you? They will not respond to efforts of young nursing home workers who try to change behaviors according to the standards of a young, productive society. The old-old return to their roots and ignore or get angry at people who will not listen to them or argue with them. They prevent vegetation by restoring the past. That is how the disoriented old-old survive.

Who are the Disoriented Old-Old?

Disoriented old-old are very old people who:
- have inflexible behavior patterns
- hold onto outworn roles
- have to grapple with unfinished feelings
- withdraw from present day reality to survive
- have significant cognitive deterioration and can no longer function intellectually to achieve insight

This population benefits from Validation.

The disoriented old-old are people who have led more or less useful, productive, satisfying lives and have no history of severe mental illness. They functioned well before being overpowered by so many losses. Ravaged by the loss of sight, hearing, recent memory, social roles, jobs, homes, and mobility, they withdraw, rather than acknowledge so many losses. Overcoming adversity through denial has worked before to help them survive life's crises. In very old age, when one crisis follows another, overloading and ganging up on them, such people retreat from reality. They have no other way of coping. Like a person lost in a storm, the disoriented very old retreat into the past to find safe shelter. The past eases present-day pain, brings back nostalgia, familiar streets, loved ones, work. There are few rewards in living in a wheelchair in a nursing home. Mrs. Kessler turns her back on young workers who want to orient her to present-day reality. She explains her return to the past in the film, *Looking for Yesterday*[20]: "I'm looking for yesterday to untangle the noodles in the mirrors of my mind." This old-old woman was diagnosed "demented". Dementia comes from the Latin "dis", meaning away from, and "mens", the mind. Hence: "out of the mind," or "mind-less." Without a mind, Mrs. Kessler, an 86-year-old Russian peasant woman, could not have been that poetic. Having lost most of her speech and logic, she moved in realms of personal feelings, freely associating words, sounds, and body movements to express herself. Bottled-up emotions spilled. The cork popped. Validation means acknowledging and respecting the behavior of very old disoriented people, who express themselves poetically, rather than logically.

Validation helps people who:
1. are old-old, aged 80-100 plus.*
2. have led relatively happy, productive lives.
3. have denied severe crises throughout their lives.
4. hold onto familiar roles.
5. show permanent damage to their brain, eyes, ears.
6. have diminished ability to move, control feelings, remember recent events.
7. meet their human needs for love, identity, and expression of feelings by using body movements and images learned early in life.

---

*Age is relative and we all grow old differently. One 90-year-old looks and acts as if she were 70. A 60-year-old behaves as if he were 90, therefore, "80-100 plus" is a generalization. There are many exceptions to the rule. I have discovered through my practice, that most people over 80 begin to suffer some degree of physical deterioration that is related to aging. They also begin to review their lives, to wrap up their experiences in order to die in peace.

8. have unresolved emotions they must express.
9. choose on a subliminal level of awareness to retreat, to avoid painful present-day reality.
10.are in the Resolution versus Vegetation stage of life, recalling the past in a struggle to resolve it. They are resolving until death.

Each person is unique and responds differently to physical and social changes that happen to everyone in old-old age. People differ more from each other in old age than in any other life stage. Categorizing disoriented old-old in one package, labeled "dementia" or the currently popular label "Alzheimer's type dementia" often leads to the use of inappropriate methods of helping them. Methods that do not work. Some very old people can roll with the punches and remain oriented despite severe damage to brain structure. Others, with similar brain damage become very disoriented.[21] The condition of the brain, is only one criterion, and does not provide enough information to make an accurate diagnosis.[22] A person's behavior in old age is influenced by his/her acquired repertoire of coping methods plus a combination of physical and social losses.

Individuals with a wide variety of behavior patterns have the best chance for success when faced with physical deterioration in old-old age.[23] These very old people do not need Validation: they validate themselves throughout life.

Validation was not developed for people who:
• are oriented
• are mentally handicapped
• have a history of mental illness
• have suffered an organic trauma (i.e.: aphasia after a stroke or fall)

These people are capable of changing their acting-out behavior. The goal of the helper is to facilitate change through confrontation, behavior modification, or insight. The goal of Validation is not to give insight or to confront because disoriented old-old people are no longer capable of cognitive thinking. However, Validation principles: empathy, warmth, respect, know your client and understand their goals, apply to most helping methods and Validation techniques can help.

Diagnostic Labeling: Dementia

Dementia is a term that was first used in the early nineteenth century by the French researchers Pinel (1745-1826) and Esquirol (1772-1840) to describe mental deterioration and idiocy caused by lesions in the brain. "Senile dementia" was seen as the progressive deterioration of the brain in aging.

Dementia is what the medical community called, an "organic brain syndrome". Until 1978, the Diagnostic and Statistical Manual of mental disorders (DSM I and DSM II), published by the American Psychiatric Association, classified dementia as a type of organic brain syndrome that is either reversible (acute) or irreversible (chronic). Acute organic brain syndromes might result from: a tumor, a metabolic disturbance, a delirium, a kidney infection, vitamin B12 deficiency, drugs, depressive psychosis, etc.

Chronic organic brain syndromes were classified as: (a) Senile dementia (age of onset over 70), and (b) Presenile dementia. The two most common types of presenile dementia were Pick's disease and Alzheimer's disease. Butler and Lewis describe these dementias as "a group of brain diseases that look like the senile dementia's seen in older people but occurring earlier, in the 40 and 50 year age groups."[24] People suffering from chronic organic brain syndrome, senile and presenile dementia types, are found to have impairment of: memory, intellectual functioning, judgment, orientation, and as having labile or shallow affects (uncontrolled emotions).

In 1981, the DSM III task force on Nomenclature and Statistics, revised the earlier diagnostic classifications for chronic organic brain syndromes for the senile and presenile demented person. At autopsy, researchers had found that the brain structures of very old people were similar to the brains of younger people diagnosed as having presenile dementia. Consequently, they saw no reason for the arbitrary distinction between senile and presenile dementias. Since that time the medical community does not make a distinction between presenile and senile dementia (also called early onset and late onset dementia). The term "organic brain syndrome" itself is used only rarely.

Diagnostic Labeling: Alzheimer's

In 1906, Alois Alzheimer, analyzing the brain of a 51 year old woman, observed that there were "remarkable changes in the neurofibrils ... and a peculiar substance in the cerebral cortex," and concluded that he was confronted with a distinctive disease process. This process was called "Alzheimer's Disease" by Alzheimer's mentor, Kraepelin. Deterioration as a result of this disease is rapid, and the earlier the onset, the more severe its course.[25] Butler and Lewis describe the decline as follows: "First, loss of cognition, then, aphasia, emotional lability, a Parkinsonism-like gait and convulsive seizures, with increasing difficulty in swallowing. Eventually utter helplessness prevails, with incontinence and marasmus. Onset takes place in the forties or fifties and an individual seldom lives longer than four or five years after the illness begins." [26] Therefore, people with Alzheimer's disease seldom reached the age of 65. They died, mainly of pneumonia or heart disease, because their immune systems were affected.

In the pre-1978 categorization, Alzheimer's Disease was one of the common forms of presenile dementia. The diagnosis was ultimately based on autopsy. If neurofibrillary plaques and tangles were found in the brain, a person was diagnosed as "Alzheimer's". Neurofibrillary tangles, first described by Alzheimer in Munich in 1906, are abnormally paired fibres, twisted filaments, in a neuron. Senile plaques, first found in 1898 by Redlich are degenerating neuron cell processes, laminated deposits of a protein called an "amyloid substance" found in the surface membrane of the brain cell.

As I explained before, similarities were noted during autopsy between the brain structures of very old people and younger individuals with Alzheimer's or presenile dementia. Blessed and associates[27] counted the number of senile plaques and neurofibrillary tangles and as a result, the distinction between presenile and senile dementia was dropped. Soon afterward, both categories were referred to as Alzheimer's. The name became synonymous with senility and almost overnight it became a common illness. In the new edition of their book *The Vanishing Mind*, Heston and White[28] describe the new situation as follows: "Alzheimer's disease and senile dementia are now regarded as one disease. And over the last few years, both terms have been discarded in formal communication in favor of dementia of the Alzheimer type, or, senile dementia of the Alzheimer type (SDAT). Pending discovery of evidence to the contrary, we assume the basic disease process is the same, regardless of age at onset."

In my view, the present attitude is confusing. In the first place, early onset Alzheimer's is a much more distinctive disease than late onset Alzheimer's. In old-old age it is quite normal to get neurofibrillary plaques and tangles in the brain. Nobel Prizewinner Carlton Gajdusek, who discovered plaques and tangles in New Guinea in 1960, wrote in 1987 that these plaques are the hallmarks of old age and that 90% of people over 90 years of age develop them in their brain. Neurologist Dennis Selkoe makes a similar point: "Most of us who live into our late seventies will develop at least a few senile plaques and neurofibrillary tangles, particularly in the hippocampus and other brain regions important for memory," and he adds: "For the most part, the distinction between a normal brain aging and Alzheimer's Disease is quantitative rather than qualitative."[29] It is important to point out that some people whose brains on autopsy show plaques and tangles have led relatively normal lives before dying. Yes, they might have become forgetful, but it is normal for very old people to forget. We begin losing brain cells in our twenties. By the time we reach our eighties, there can be significant loss of recent, or short-term memory. This is a normal part of aging, not a disease.

There is a another reason why it is confusing to lump early and late onset Alzheimer's together. The anatomical structures that change the brain and are seen at autopsies, are not the sole orchestrators of behavior at very old age. The condition of the brain is rarely the answer to the behavior of the living old person.[30] Scientists that are doing brain research do not work with *living* old people, they study cadavers. They do not hear an 88-year-old-woman say, as she looks under tables and chairs, "I'm looking for yesterday. I have to untangle the noodles in the mirrors of my mind." They don't see the behavioral differences between early and late onset dementia. The behavior of those with early onset dementia typically follow the Alzheimer's model. Those with late onset dementia are what I call the disoriented old-old. Their behavior, speech, gait, and expressions of human needs are different.   They respond to

Validation techniques by not withdrawing, and their speech and gait improve. (See the research studies describing the results of Validation on page 37.) These people can often be helped without medication. Early onset Alzheimer's patients, on the other hand, continue to deteriorate to the stage of vegetation. The course of the disease is progressive regardless of Validation interventions. The Validation care-giver cannot predict the behavior of early onset Alzheimer's patients. Validation may restore some social interaction for a moment, but the next moment the patient may become violent, wander away or withdraw without motivation. Unlike the immediate recognition response of the old-old, the eyes of an early onset Alzheimer's patient usually remain unfocused, blank, staring without recognition.

Validation Workers

This section describes the attitudes and qualities that are needed in order to practice Validation effectively. The techniques are secondary. Most importantly, the Validation worker must accept that the disoriented old person's withdrawal inward can be a normal part of aging, that their return to the past is a survival method, a healing process and a way of easing the blows dealt by aging. Old age is not a disease. The Validation worker accepts the physical deterioration of very old people and knows that their life goals differ from those of young, healthy individuals.

Goals for Younger Individuals

- Think. Produce. Use your head. Figure things out.
- Communicate clearly. Use well-chosen dictionary words.
- Keep track of clock-time. Avoid daydreaming.
- Control your emotions.
- Confine wishful thinking to coffee breaks, dreams, holidays.
- Conform to society's rules.
- Become "somebody." Work to achieve success.

Goals for Disoriented Old-old

- Retreat from painful present day feelings of uselessness.
- Relive past pleasures.
- Relieve boredom by stimulating sensory memories.
- Resolve unfinished conflicts by expressing feelings.

Validation workers, or V/Ws, are non-judgmental, they accept and respect the wisdom of old people. The V/W never walks in front of the old-old trying to convince them of the present. Nor does he or she patronize the old-old by walking behind them, pretending to agree with them. Sure of their own reality, they can afford to walk beside the mal- and disoriented. V/Ws are always honest. Disoriented old-old people recognize pretense. The deaf will "hear" a snicker. The blind will "see" a smirk. They know the difference between the put down pat and warm, respectful human contact. On a subliminal level of awareness the old-old know the truth, like a sleeper who unconsciously swats a mosquito, they are unaware and do not want to be made aware.

The V/Ws mission is to help the disoriented old-old accomplish *their* final life task: to die in peace. To do that the disoriented old-old need to be heard by a trusted listener who respects the feelings of old people, and knows that each feeling is genuine. Imprisoned emotions demand to be released in this quest for resolution; to see the light of day during this final life stage . The V/W knows that when human feelings are acknowledged and validated, the old-old disoriented feel better. Their stress is relieved. Listening does not "feed the fantasy." Listening with empathy reduces anxiety.

The disoriented old-old person is not a child. The V/W is not a parent and does not use "parent" words, such as "should," or "must."[31] The V/W does not punish, threaten or patronize. They do not shut off the old person's feelings nor force expression of feelings, respectful of disoriented old-old's privacy. V/Ws tune into their client; pick up rhythms; listen to verbal clues; and observe non-verbal clues. The V/W puts feelings into words to affirm them and to give dignity to the very old person. Validation means respecting the disoriented old-old who have lived a lifetime and acknowledging their wisdom. V/Ws do not expect all disoriented old-old to act alike, but respect the unique differences in all people.

The Validation Worker uses empathy. We do not judge three-year-olds by our adult standards. All of us have been three years old and can step into their shoes. We do not call teenagers psychotic when they act out their feelings. All of us have been teenagers and know that they are in a stage of rebellion, trying to find their own identity.

None of us, however, have been old-old. It's much harder to step into the wheelchair of a 90-year-old man who pounds his fist, cannot see clearly, hear well, move or remember his name, and certainly not ours. It's much harder to move to his rhythms and see with his eyes. He cannot see his hand. He sees a hammer and a nail. This old man was an expert carpenter, his father and grandfather were also carpenters. He learned to pound a nail straight as a child. As an old man he sits and pounds to restore his identity. The Validation worker has empathy for him. We can step into the lives of the old-old, because we too have suffered losses.

Have you ever felt the momentary panic of losing your bearings when driving alone at night in a storm, with no one to ask directions? Then you've felt the bewilderment of the disoriented old-old who forget where they are. Have you experienced numbness of a limb, blurry vision, impaired hearing, felt the loss of someone or something you loved, the anxiety of losing a job, a home, a physical capacity? If you have felt generalized fear, rage, jealousy, guilt, grief, and love, then you can share human feelings with disoriented old-old.

The Validation Worker is a super-adult who has achieved adult intimacy, identity, has separated from authority and is able to express herself without fear of rejection. V/Ws are responsible for their own feelings even when they are uncomfortable. They can accept raw, gut emotions from disoriented old-old and mirror them with empathy. When an old woman rocks, crying,"Ma ma ma ma," the V/W acknowledges the old woman's need for her mother, using the appropriate Validation techniques. There is genuine eye contact between the V/W and the disoriented old-old woman, who no longer turns to the past to find love. She has found it with the V/W.

Care-givers who cannot share intimate feelings with disoriented very old people who freely express them, should not be working with them. People who communicate only on verbal, intellectual, controlled, logical levels will be unable to use the Validation techniques with empathy. They will be very uncomfortable, will turn away from the disoriented old-old or sedate them. Not everyone should do Validation. Workers who cannot accept strong emotions can work well with oriented and maloriented very old people who do control their feelings.

Validation workers are superhuman, because they can empathize with very old disoriented people, and respect their feelings as valid, without knowing *why* the old person acts that way. Super-adult V/Ws do not expect the entire nursing home staff to practice Validation. They respect the fact that some staff may not be able to cross the street to walk in the footsteps of the disoriented old-old. Some staff members expect the older person to do the crossing, to be aware of present day reality. The wise old person will ignore this staff member saying to himself, "I wait for the one that doesn't argue with me."

The Validation Worker is not an Analyst.

The V/W knows that the old-old disoriented have lost the cognitive capacity for insight. They can no longer relate their emotions to intellect or "figure out" the reasons behind their feelings in order to change their behavior. They have lost the capacity for the "AHA!" - the sudden realization. With empathy, the V/W sees with the eyes, hears with the ears, and mirrors the body rhythms of the old-old people, in order to help them meet their need for identity, love, and validation of their raw emotions.

The V/W knows that the disoriented old-old will **never completely resolve their unfinished life tasks. They will be resolving them until they die.** They can never achieve sufficient insight to completely change their behavior. They need a nurturing, validating person who respects their feelings, listens, affirms, and walks beside them on the streets of the past.

Burn Out and Feelings of Failure[32]

Feelings of failure occur when workers expect disoriented old-old people to behave according to the workers' standards: speak clearly, control emotions, make daily progress, obey rules, listen, or communicate with words. If the worker can accept the physical deterioration of the old-old disoriented person they will rarely experience burn out or feelings of failure. Burn out results from unrealistic expectations, when workers forget that the old-old disoriented will not and cannot remember names, the time of day or the date. They will remember a genuine touch, warm eye contact, and a nurturing voice-tone. Their eyes will light, they smile for the first time in months and the worker feels pleasure in inspiring a life. One moment of genuinely sharing makes up for many difficult hours with residents.

Ways to Prevent Burn out:
- have realistic expectations
- set realistic goals for each old-old person
- acknowledge and chart your progress
- get support from wherever you can: family members, staff, volunteers, coworkers
- organize a Validation team.

Change comes in small fragments, but it does come. Three months of consistent Validation will bring significant improvements in behavior.[33] Measuring change by using the Validation Evaluation of Progress chart on page 114, will help workers see their progress. Families can participate in Validation by attending regular family workshops. When family and staff share Validation they support each other and everyone enjoys the pleasure of the wisdom, poetry and intimacy that are part of disorientation in old-old age.

In any institution, the administrator's understanding and approval of Validation goals is vital, especially when the V/W begins to form a Validation group. Forming one depends upon the support of the entire staff: housekeeping, dietitians, social service, nursing personnel and recreation workers. If the administrator and director of nursing do not support Validation, the nursing aide may not be instructed to take each group member to the toilet before the meeting, the meeting room may not be available, and staff members might interrupt and take individuals out of the group, destroying its continuity. Lack of staff support will burn out the V/W who wants to begin a group, however, individual Validation can still be practiced.

A Validation team can include just a few people or as many as an entire institution. Through regular meetings, you can evaluate your progress, share your experiences, express your frustrations and gain insights into your own behavior. A team gives you support and alleviates isolation.

Results of Research Studies

Disoriented old-old people respond to Validation. Change in behavior is slow and fluctuates from day to day, but permanent change does occur.

These are some of the measurable results that you can expect:
* they sit more erect
* their eyes open
* increased social controls
* less crying, pacing, pounding (repetitive behaviors)
* less aggressive
* less need for chemical and physical restraints
* increased verbal communication
* increased non-verbal communication
* improved gait

Here are the notable results that are not measurable:
* resolving unfinished life tasks
* reduced anxiety
* less withdrawal
* a greater sense of self-worth
* the assumption of familiar social roles through Validation groups
* increased awareness of reality
* restoration of a sense of humor

My study at the Montefiore Home for the Aged in 1971, showed that after five years of Validation, thirty organically brain-damaged, disoriented old-old people improved in many ways. They became less incontinent, there was less negative behavior (crying, pounding, hitting), and more positive behavior (smiling, talking, helping others). People became more aware of external reality, they talked outside of group meetings, and were more content.[34]

In 1976, also at The Montefiore Home for the Aged in Cleveland, I compared four years of transcriptions of two groups. One was the "coffee klatch group," of oriented, very old nursing home residents with physical disabilities. The other was the "Tuesday group" of disoriented, very old residents in the same nursing home. This comparison showed that denial is the common defense against stress for the disoriented old-old who withdraw to the past.[35]

In 1980, Stan Alprin, a Cleveland researcher, took a very different approach to the assessment of Validation. He examined its impact therapist's attitude and behavior as well as its effect on the disoriented very old nursing home resident. Alprin obtained quantified data with regard to behavioral changes of residents and staffs in nursing home settings in 16 homes throughout the United States who were using Validation with disoriented very old residents. He surveyed directors, activity personnel and social workers. He reported: "The evidence obtained thus far would suggest very strongly [that there were] many positive changes in behavior of resident groups following Validation...Shifts in staff behavior were in a positive direction."[36] Those shifts included: more trust between nursing staff and residents, less aggressive behavior exhibited by the residents, less staff turnover.

In her Master's thesis for the University of Akron, Ohio, Marlene Peoples compared the effects of Validation with Reality Orientation in a 225 bed nursing home in 1982. She used standardized statistical tools to assess the degree of confusion in small groups. There were "qualitative improvements in behavior for seven of the ten subjects in the Validation group compared with three of the eight subjects in the Reality Orientation group. Attendance at the Validation group was better. Validation produced significant improvement in behavior..., whereas Reality Orientation produced no significant difference."[37] I received other studies that corroborate this finding.

In 1986, Paul A. Fritz, a professor at the University of Toledo, analyzed the effectiveness of Validation on speech patterns of cognitively impaired very old residents of nursing homes in Toledo, Ohio. He wrote: "I found that Validation made a significant improvement on the elders' speech patterns. I used a computer program which measures the number of verbs, nouns, prepositions, etc. that a person uses in recorded conversation. I found that the categories of Malorientation and Time Confusion [two of the four stages of disorientation as defined later in this book] showed a significant increase in fluency levels and in lucidness."[38]

James T. Dietch MD of the Irvine Medical Center in California, and others, published their study, "Adverse Effects of Reality Orientation" in 1989. It states: "This validation approach was found to be more effective than application of Reality Orientation (RO)...Validation Therapy differs radically from RO and appears to be a useful approach in some patients with dementia... Staff may benefit by avoiding the repetitive frustration of attempting to reorient patients in areas they are incapable of changing. Greater staff awareness of the individual psychological and emotional needs of dementia patients will result in improved therapeutic care."[39]

In Australia, Colin Sharp PhD, research and evaluation consultant, compared identical populations in two nursing homes, one used Validation and the other did not. In 1989, he found that both staff and residents benefitted from Validation. There was a reduction of withdrawal and more positive interaction and socialization. The efficacy of Validation was manifested in the Validation home.[40] Ian Morton and Christine Bleathman, nurses at Maudsley Hospital in London concur with Sharp's findings in their 1991 study.[41]

In 1991, Dr. Jean Prentczynski, a French physician and researcher, carried out a study similar to Sharp's at the Hospital Sebastopol in Reims, France, with similar results. "There was an increased resolving of their conflicts and reduced anxiety, less suspicion and increased trust with staff."[42]

As of 1992, over 70,000 persons have been trained to use Validation in homes, nursing homes, hospitals and communities, in North America, Europe, and Australia.

How to Prevent Your Own Disorientation

Helen Thomas lives alone. She is 76 years old. When her husband died of cancer three years ago, Helen dried a few tears, shuffled her ambivalent guilt and grief, stomped on her feelings and went on living. She found a volunteer job in a library near her home. Now she shelves books as well as her feelings. She never asks her children for help, never needs help - she thinks. Whenever hardships hit, Helen hits back, never gives in to her fears. She always controls her emotions, always pulls herself together.

It's 5:00 a.m. Helen always wakes up at 5:00 a.m. She opens her eyes - but she can't see. Everything is black. Helen gropes for the night-lamp, turns it on, but there's no light. Did all the fuses blow? Helen blinks away tears and tries to shut down her anxiety. The more she tries to stop the flood of fear, the more she panics. Her heart pounds. Her hands and face are covered with sweat. She feels nauseous. Terror takes over. Helen is blind. She shrieks, "Help! I can't see. Help!" The neighbors call 911. A rescue squad takes her to the emergency room in a nearby hospital. Still screaming, Helen gets the latest tranquilizing medication. Within two weeks, Helen is placed in a nursing home, unaware of the present time or place, her head slumped on her chest in a wheelchair, her eyes closed, hands limp, mouth open, barely breathing - a living dead person.

The diagnosis? Helen is given the standard test to determine her mental status. She can not count backwards by ten; does not know the name of the President of the United States; can no longer perform simple tasks of daily living; her emotions are labile, spilling out without control; and a CAT scan reveals the possibility of small strokes that have destroyed Helen's brain tissue over the last few years. Diagnosis: "Dementia of the Alzheimer's Type."

How could Helen have prevented her disorientation? With one hundred billion brain cells, and quadrillions of possible connections, a younger Helen could have gained insight, struggled to know herself, to become aware of her pattern of denying unpleasant feelings. She could have developed new ways of coping when hard times hit, but she didn't.

Facing unpleasant feelings is scary. Trying an unknown path

is risky. Learning to walk in a unfamiliar direction can lead to panic. We have to be painfully honest with ourselves, risk making mistakes, get used to shame and despair before we can perfect new ways of living. The better we know ourselves, the less likely we are to fall apart in very old age. The more self-aware, the easier it is to cast off worn-out, rusty ways of coping.

Steps for Coping with Aging:

- know your preferred sense*
- pay attention to your body
- find a coping mechanism for crisis situations
- keep resolving your unfinished life tasks and issues
- accept what you can't change and respect yourself.

* In infancy, we are overwhelmed by a battery of sensory information. We are nursing. Our mother *feels* warm and soft. We *taste* the sweet milk, *hear* the sound of her voice, *smell* her familiar scent, *see* her lips and her eyes. Too many sensations for a two week-old-infant. To keep our balance, we blot out some of the senses, and concentrate on one. This becomes our preferred sense. As we mature, we use all our senses, but use our preferred sense most of the time, developing and honing it. Later in life, we rely on our preferred sense to tell us what is happening in the outside world; to verify our perceptions; to correct any misconceptions we may have about the environment; to adjust our inner reality to what's happening out there.

Here is Helen's life revised. As a girl, she relied on her vision for pure enjoyment of living. She loved painting. Her oil canvases decorated the living room. She used to smear colors, splashing one into the other. When Helen was about 10, she fashioned multicolored dresses for her paper dolls. As a teenager, she would wander in the woods watching the grayish-brown-purple leaves flirt with the wind. Visits to the Art Museum were pure joy. She reveled in the colors of the Dutch Masters. As a mother, Helen dressed herself and her children with care, always matching colors.

As an adult, knowing that seeing is her preferred sense, Helen prepares for aging and possible vision loss by perfecting her other senses. She could take a Yoga class to get in touch with her kinesthetic sense, develop breathing techniques, learn about her body movements, and to cope with internal and external stress. She could sign up for a dance class to learn how to move with ease, stretch her muscles, stand straight, hold herself together by aligning her body. She should learn what to do in moments of stress, how to survive momentary panic. When she is lost while driving in a strange city, in the middle of the night, with her little boy crying, and no gas station in sight, Helen could overcome her terror. It takes Helen no more than two minutes to follow these...

Steps for Centering:[43]

1. Focus on a spot about two inches below the waist. This is your center. The center of your gravity.

2. Inhale deeply through the nose, filling your body with the breath.

3. Exhale through the mouth.

4. Stop all inner dialogue and pay attention to your breathing.

5. Mentally follow your breath from your center up in an arc back to your nose.

6. Take in the breath and fill your body with it.

7. Wash the breath out at the center.

At 50, Helen needs bifocals. She prepares for vision loss by developing her other senses. She takes a class in music. She learns to play the piano, attends more concerts. She refines her sense of taste and smell, studied the art of wine tasting, becomes a gourmet cook.

At 60, it takes Helen much longer than usual to adjust to the dark. She wonders why her hands get clammy, her eyes narrow, her heart pounds whenever she is suddenly, unexpectedly faced with the dark. Helen asks her family, at a Thanksgiving dinner, if they remember an incident when she was locked in the dark. Helen's brother chuckles with sadistic glee. When he was five and Helen was four, he locked her in the closet. "You could hear Helen shriek for five blocks." Their mother rescued Helen within minutes, but she never forgot the terror of the dark. Her body remembers each detail. Today, at the Thanksgiving meal, her stomach retches at the vivid memory. Similar feelings march through time. A dark movie theater in present time triggers an early memory of being locked in a dark closet fifty years ago. Helen tells her brother how she felt long ago, and how she feels now. In acknowledging her terror of the dark, Helen washes it away. She has added a new insight; a new connection cements in her brain. The "AHA!" brings a "HA-HA!" She feels relief, faces her fears and overcomes them.

At age 63, Helen begins to feel pain in her neck and shoulder. Her body finally rebels, giving her information about herself. In group therapy she realizes that she has always been a martyr. She was a good, little girl, never risking the displeasure of her parents. As a wife, she never said no to her husband and had six children without a murmur. Helen always wanted to go to college, but she had to wait until her youngest child was grown. After years of denial, Helen now consciously changes her ways of responding to others and becomes honest with herself. She learns to say "no" to her husband, her children, and her 90 year old mother, without pangs of guilt or fear of being abandoned. When Helen feels sick to her stomach, or has a pain in her neck, or a tightening in her shoulder, Helen centers, realigns her muscles, and faces her anger or her fear.

To age successfully:

1. Face each life task as it comes. If you miss a task, go back and tackle it before you reach old-old age. Put your life in order as you go!

2. Learn to play lots of keys on the piano of your life. When one key goes flat, play another. If you begin to go deaf, develop your sense of sight, taste, touch and smell. If your job goes, get involved in volunteer work. Roll with the punches. Expand your coping repertoire while you're young.

Validation in a Nutshell

Disoriented old-old lose controls; lose the will to control; lose their defenses to deny feelings. Their feelings spill without control. In old-old age, they gain the wisdom to freely express feelings in order to resolve them. The Validation worker does not explore feelings that are not expressed. The worker does not analyze feelings that are expressed. Unlike younger neurotic or psychotic patients, disoriented old-old cannot be forced to face their feelings. The worker cannot "allow" or "forbid" feelings. Disoriented old-old, with intuitive wisdom of age, will not listen to a younger worker who tells them what to do. They are not children. They will not learn new behaviors. They are summing-up, not growing up. They freely express feelings to resolve them. They are not living to conform to the young worker's expectations of behavior. The worker can modify behaviors of young-old who can return to the community. Old-old will continue to express feelings regardless of the worker. If someone listens genuinely, the feelings often subside. The old person is validated by a trusted listener. The worker never pretends; never forces feelings; never makes fun of feelings.

Validation Principles:

I. Behavioral
   A. Early, well-established learning stays. When recent memory fades, early learning surfaces. (Homeostasis)
   B. An event in the present can trigger an early memory. Past and present become one.
   C. A physical loss in the present can activate a vivid memory of an early emotion. Example: Loss of eyesight at 90 triggers the terror of being locked up in a dark room when five years old.

II. Developmental
   A. Each stage of life has a different task. Human beings must face each task and struggle to accomplish it. Life tasks are rarely resolved. We continue resolving until we die. A task ignored demands to be heard in a later stage. The ignored

task wants to be "put back in place."

B. Those who live to very old age with a backpack of squelched tasks enter a final life stage: Resolution versus Vegetation. The old-old struggle to express unfinished tasks to make peace before death.

C. Physical losses (eyesight, hearing, recent memory) help the old-old to blot out the present and restore the past.

III. Psychological

A. Ignored feelings fester, waiting in the dark.

B. Exposed to the light of day, they lose strength.

C. Exquisite listening with empathy (Validating) relieves the emotional burden. Acknowledged, shared, and validated, a feeling can go away.

D. Ignoring the very old person's emotions does not modify their behavior. If no one listens to them their behavior worsens, or they withdraw to vegetation.

46

PART TWO

THE STAGES OF DISORIENTATION

Maloriented and disoriented old-old have entered the final life stage, Resolution versus Vegetation. They have never achieved what Erikson calls integrity. I have divided this population into four distinct stages. These stages can be identified by their physical and psychological characteristics. Each stage is a further retreat from reality, a slow physical regression. Don't get hardening of the categories, people move from stage to stage sometimes within five minutes. Usually, however, they are in one stage most of the time. A man can be oriented at 8:00 a.m., and at 3:00 p.m. he has to go home to feed his horses and milk the cows.

Stage One: Malorientation - unhappily oriented to reality
Stage Two: Time Confusion - loss of cognitive capacities
Stage Three: Repetitive Motion - repetitive movements replace
         speech
Stage Four: Vegetation - total retreat inward

In order to understand the old-old in these four stages, one needs to understand their use of symbols.

Symbols - Tickets to the Past

A symbol is an object or person in the present, that represents a significant object or person from the past.[44] A soft toy can become a mother's hug, a cigarette, the nipple. We all use symbols in art, poetry, and dreams. With our cognitive ability intact, we are able to connect two things or two people, compare them without losing their identity. We can think in metaphors. "My hand is a baby" is a poet's way of comparing two things. The poet knows that the hand is soft *like* a baby. The hand becomes a symbol of the baby. Maloriented and disoriented old-old also use symbols. The maloriented use present-day objects and people to trigger past emotions to express them. A maloriented woman who has suppressed anger towards her mother, accuses her daughter, who is now her care-giver, "You're neglecting your children. A mother who loves her children doesn't leave them alone with a babysitter." The old woman has substituted her daughter for her mother. Disoriented old-old people have lost the cognitive ability to keep objects or people separate. They have lost the "as-if." The hand that feels soft like a baby, *becomes* the baby. This woman lovingly strokes her hand-baby. The symbols in both cases refer to people or objects in the past that were real. They did exist.

Symbols used by psychotic adults may look like those of a maloriented or disoriented old-old person. Maloriented old-old are frequently diagnosed as having paranoid hallucinations or delusions. A psychotic person fabricates imagined symbols from inner fears. Their hallucinations or delusions are pathological, unfounded perceptions of reality and those people need help. Their symbols do not relate to the loss of intellectual functioning, nor are they healing themselves in a final life stage.

When the outside world blurs because of failing eyesight, diminished hearing and loss of tactile sensations, it becomes easy, and in this final life stage, natural to replace present-day objects and people with the past. Maloriented people often use present-day authority figures (administrator, bus driver, handyman, head nurse, etc.) to express bottled up anger at their parents. "The administrator never listens to me, he's never around, his door is always closed. When I try to talk to him he's always too busy. But he has time for everyone else." The world of disoriented people has a storehouse of symbols.[45] A napkin becomes the earth. Neatly, carefully, meticulously, an old-old woman in Stage Two folds, caresses, pats, croons, kissing each fold. She is patting herself in place, putting herself in order on this earth. She belongs, is happy. Her world is in order. The napkin enables her to express her longing to be loved, enfolded, warm and safe.

After 35 years of working with maloriented and disoriented people around the world, I have found the following typical symbols.

Universal Symbols and What They Can Mean

Jewelry, clothing	Worth, identity
Shoe	Container, womb, male or female

	sex symbol
Purse	Female sex symbol, vagina, identity
Cane or fist	Penis, potency, power
Soft furniture	Safety, mother, home
Hard furniture	Father, God
Napkin, tissue, flat object	Earth, belonging, vagina, identity
Food	Love, mother
Drink from a glass	Male power, potency
Any receptacle	Womb
Picking the nose	Sexual pleasure
Playing with feces	Early childhood pleasures

A Few Typical Personal Symbols Used by Disoriented Old-Old:

A hand	A baby
A finger	A parent, feet to walk, children to walk with
A cloth	Important papers, dough for baking, children's clothes
The arm of a chair	A street
Open space	A hallway at home, heaven, hope
Button, pebble	Nourishment, love
Clucking sound	Safety, joy
Rocking movement	Mother, motherhood, safety, joy
Liquid	Male power
Strong chair	Penis, man, husband, sex
Fork, knife	Anger
Handle	Penis
Low voice	Male person
Spoon or curved object	Woman, female sex
Sock, shoe	Child, dressing a child, or a sexual organ
Removable piece of clothing	Sexual act, freedom, defiance
A nursing home floor	A neighborhood
The hallway	A street in the neighborhood
A wheelchair	A car, bike, carriage

I have found these symbols to be universal, regardless of race, religion, culture, or sex. These same symbols are used in Australia, the Netherlands, France, Belgium, Norway, Austria, Canada, Germany, Finland, and the United States.

Stage One: Malorientation

These people hold onto socially prescribed rules with one exception, they need to express past conflicts in disguised forms. They use people in the present as symbols[46] for people from the past: an old-old woman claims her roommate is stealing her underwear. The roommate symbolizes a sister, of whom she was very jealous. A woman who never expressed her sexual desires claims a man is hiding under her bed.

Feelings are denied. Speech, reason and rational thinking are very important. The maloriented person values cool, clear judgment and control, often resenting touch and close eye contact. They keep track of time, think things through, put items into their proper place and keep order. They are ashamed when caught slipping up by occasionally forgetting, repeating a statement or story, or mistaking identities. They confabulate, use made up experiences to cover their gaps in memory, and deny them. Feeling old and useless in an institution or alone at home they sense, this is punishment for past behavior, and say, "Someone is poisoning" their food. Food is a symbol for love. Bitter, alone and unloved they claim, "Someone is stealing" their possessions. They feel robbed by old age and in childhood they felt robbed by sisters, brothers, parents, who "stole" their dignity. Similar feelings march through time, attracting each other like magnets.

To justify themselves or deny their strong emotions as they have throughout their lives, they blame and accuse others. When their partner dies, they never feel grief or guilt, but blame the doctors. They resent retirement, but instead of expressing the anger, they blame the boss for being prejudiced against older people. When they loose their hair due to normal aging, they blame the beautician or barber. To maintain control in a battle against the loss of controls, they hoard. Fearful of increasing loss, they store up whatever they can - oranges, safety pins, tissues, cups, sugar packets, salt, newspapers, ribbons, to protect themselves against future losses. No one will persuade them otherwise. "Convinced against their will, they hold the same opinion still." The need to justify the past is stronger than "truth." Their deepest fears are projected onto others in order to maintain equilibrium. They need to defend themselves, need their cover-ups. Don't strip them of their defenses, their dignity. They need these types of behavior to survive. Through them they express their feelings without having to expose them to the harsh light of reality. They need a trusting relationship with a nurturing, respectful authority who will not argue with them, who understands and doesn't judge. They need Validation.

Physical Characteristics of Malorientation:
- Eyes are clear and focused.
- Stance is rigid.
- Movement in space (even in a wheelchair or with a walker) is definite, sustained, precise.
- Face and body muscles are tight.
- Jaw often juts out.
- Fingers and hands are often pointing. The arms often folded.
- Lips are tight.
- Breathing is shallow.
- Voice tone is clear, harsh, whining or shrill.[47]
- Often clutch a coat, cane, or purse.
- Cognitive ability is relatively intact, can categorize, have a concept of clock time.
- Read, write, figure. Use dictionary words.
- Losses to sight, hearing, tactile sensation, mobility are relatively minor.

Psychological Characteristics of Malorientation:
- Need to express bottled up emotions.
- Hold onto present reality.
- Want to understand and to be understood.
- Play games with rules.
- Are aware of occasional confusion.
- Deny confusion or confabulate (make up stories to fill in memory gaps)
- Hear, see, talk and move fairly well. Listen.

- Resist change.
- Deny feelings (such as loneliness, rage, fear, sexual longings.)
- Blame others when losses become great.
- Can not achieve insight into the reasons behind behavior.
- Want validation from authority: staff, friends, family, doctors, etc.
- Get furious at others who cannot or will not use self-control.
- Resent touch and intimacy. Do not want their vulnerability exposed.
- Use a "kinesphere", an invisible circle that surrounds every person. Maloriented people feel protected by an inviolable sphere of about 20 inches around the body.

Stage Two: Time Confusion

Too many physical and social losses create the straw that breaks the camel's back. Further loss of eyesight, hearing, mobility, tactile sensation, smell, taste and cognitive capacity make it easy for people to retreat. Time-confused people can no longer deny the losses, no longer hang onto reality. They give up trying to hold onto chronological order and retreat inward. Instead of tracking minutes, they track memories. They lose track of present time and trace their life-time. One feeling triggers another. A person or object in the present is the symbol - the ticket to yesterday. A familiar movement is the transportation vehicle. Vivid (eidetic) images supply the horsepower. Blurry hearing and eyesight, plus little recent memory are reasons for the trip. Uselessness and loneliness cost a lot. Futility is a high price for awareness of reality.

Brain damage affects the control centers. Time-confused people: lose adult controls, communications skills, social skills, no longer conform to dress codes or social rules, and miss stimulation from others because they are frequently ignored or isolated. They become incontinent physically as well as emotionally.

In time confusion, the disoriented old-old person returns to basic, universal feelings: love, hate, fear of separation, struggle for identity. These emotions are expressed by all the disoriented old-old people in hundreds of nursing homes all over the world. Universal feelings are the heart of fairy tales, classics, folk tales, and myths.[48] The Validation worker can empathize with the helpless rage of sleeping beauties who have suffered the sting of the tranquilizing needle, drug, or restraint. The V/W understands their fear of separation, shouts for identity, and wailing for help when they face the unknown. The care-giver acknowledges the universal fear of the dark and death, the longing for belonging, for meaning, for love and they do not dismiss the cries of disoriented old-old people with, "They only want attention."

A maloriented person becomes time-confused after an onslaught of losses. Had the maloriented been validated, they might not have retreated. Validation would have kept them communicating, expressing and resolving despite the increasing losses. For example: a maloriented man is moved into a nursing home when his son can no longer tolerate his father's accusing, blaming behavior. The move leads to a sudden withdrawal into time confusion. With Validation, his fears could have been expressed within the maloriented boundaries. The man needn't have been placed in a nursing home or become time-confused. He could have remained in his own home despite his accusations, which would have decreased with Validation.

Physical Characteristics of Time Confusion:
• Muscles are loose. Graceful movements.
• Eyes are clear, but often unfocused, gazing into the distance.
• Breath is slow, sustained.
• Movement in space is slow, indirect, and often questioning: Which way?
• Speech is slow.
• Hand gestures match the feelings, often questioning.
• Voice tone is low and even, seldom whiny or harsh.
• Shoulders tend to slump forward, neck down. The person often shuffles when walking.

Psychological Characteristics of Time Confusion:
• Reality is blurred because of increased deterioration of rational thinking, eyesight and hearing.
• Capable of expressing emotions, but do not remember facts.
• Metaphoric thinking is lost. They do not put people or objects in

accepted categories, cannot compare.
* A lifetime of experience has given them crystallized wisdom; they return to an intuitive knowing.[49]
* Know who is genuine and who pretends.
* Remember sensory, pleasurable feelings from childhood.
* Do NOT listen to people in the present.
* Forget recent events, but have excellent recall for past events that hold strong feelings.
* The energy focus is to resolve past unfinished conflicts, to trigger feelings of usefulness and pleasure.
* Use unique word forms from early memories, are poetic and creative. See the "Symofile" story on page 25.
* Cannot play games with rules (such as Bingo).
* Tell time by personal feelings, not by the clock. Time is measured by lifetime experiences.

    Example: A person is hungry for love. Love = food. They demand food right after lunch.

* Use pronouns without specific references. "He" can refer to God, father, devil, self-identity, the world, authority, masculinity, etc.
* There is an increasing use of symbols to represent people and events remembered from the past. They think in (eidetic) images, rather than words.
* Respond to nurturing touch and eye contact with decreased stress.
* Often lose the ability to sing on key.
* Often retain the ability to read, but lose the ability to write.
* Have a short attention span.
* Hear sounds clearly from the distant past, especially when they are deaf.
* Lose adult controls, often demanding immediate satisfaction of instincts such as sex, love and food.

Stage Three: Repetitive Motion

Individuals in Stage Two who cannot resolve their feelings by sharing them with another person who validates them, often retreat to basic pre-language movements and sounds to nurture themselves and to work through unfinished conflicts from earlier times. Body parts become symbols and movements replace words in this stage of disorientation. A person who feels tied up, dresses and undresses repeatedly to feel free. One who feels emotionally hungry eats chalk to relieve the longing. Others who are angry, pound until their fury decreases.

Each person has a different concept of which feelings are "bad", depending on their parents' concept of "bad" behavior. In old-old age, they have the wisdom to express these feelings to resolve the conflict. Shame, guilt, sexual desire or anger lie buried for a lifetime, hidden, safely controlled. Decades later, in disoriented old-old age, they come to the surface again. A man in Stage Three drops his pants. He wants to prove he is virile for the first time in his life. Or, he finally expresses rage at parents who punished his sexuality when he was an adolescent.

Feelings that have been stopped up for a lifetime, now overflow. The plug is gone. Anger at rigid rules, shame for having "messed up" during toilet training, guilt for not performing at the right time in the right place for the right person, are expressed in agitated motion before they cross the finish line.

In Stage Three, speech becomes non-intellectual; a function of the sensory pleasure of tongue, teeth, and lips making sounds. "When logical, secondary-learned speech goes, they return to 'primal linguistic patterns.'"[50] [51] Alone, isolated, wanting their mother, they bring her back by making well-established sounds from their early childhood, "Ma ma ma ma." The movement of the lips smacking together becomes mother. The person is no longer alone, he has brought back his mother as the infant does when it first learns to speak.

Body movement can transport some people into the past. An old-old woman rocks because it triggers the memory of being rocked by her mother. The nurse touching the old woman gently, symbolizes mother. The touch becomes the mother's touch, relieving anxiety and restoring safety. With one touch, the woman travels back in time 80 years. A woman in Stage Three uses a sock to represent her son because she used to wash her son's socks. She is going home in her imagination. The sock reminds her of her son, the sock *becomes* her

son.
      With vivid images,[52] they change a nursing home into a productive work place and travel to the past. A chair that feels strong, like a father, becomes "Daddy," an old woman's hand becomes her baby. Individuals who look or sound like friends, relatives or colleagues from the past, become those people, regardless of age or sex. Having lost awareness of their body in space and using vivid memories, these people "walk" or "dance" in their wheelchairs without moving their feet. With careful, familiar hand movements they pantomime, filling in the missing things or people with vivid memory. In all parts of the world, I have found that disoriented old-old use symbols and movements to travel to the past. In Casper, Wyoming a man uses his fingers to drill oil; in Northern Minnesota they chop trees; in farming areas they milk imaginary cows, skillfully moving fingers and hands to recreate the memory. They work in old-old age as they worked for a lifetime. Now they work to survive the bleak present.

Awareness of painful reality causes further retreat into the past. Drugs and restraints often increase withdrawal. Validation through confirmation and sharing feelings in a nurturing relationship often keeps Stage Two from progressing to Stage Three. Validation gives a person in time confusion, moments of rational thinking. It relieves stress and the need to return to the past.

Physical Characteristics of Repetitive Motion:
- Sway or dance.
- Sing but cannot talk in sentences.
- Make humming, clucking, moaning sounds.
- Muscles are loose, move gracefully, but are unaware of movements.
- Are incontinent.
- Eyes are often closed or not focused.
- Cry frequently.
- Fingers and hands pound, beat, tap, button and unbutton.
- Pace.
- Repeat one sound and/or movement over and over.
- Breathing is steady, rhythmic and even.
- Voice is low, melodic.

- Have moments of super physical strength when grasping for love or expressing anger.
- Are ambidextrous when freeing self of restraints.
- Cannot read or write.
- Can sing an early learned song from beginning to end.

Psychological Characteristics of Repetitive Motion:
- Need for speech is lost through disuse.
- Constant movement keep people alive, give pleasure, control anxiety, relieve boredom and confirm existence.
- Ability and desire to think is lost.
- Repetitive sounds stimulate, reassure and help resolve feelings.
- If motivated, can restore well-established social roles.
- Have increasing loss of self-awareness and awareness of their body in space (kinesthetic).
- Unless motivated, shut out external stimuli.
- Have energy for dancing and singing, but much less for talking or thinking.
- Have a short attention span. Cannot focus on more than one person or object at a time.
- Do not respond unless stimulated through a combination of close contact, nurturing touch, voice tone, and eye contact.
- Resigned to isolation and self-stimulation.
- Have the wisdom to try to resolve unfinished conflicts through movement.
- Remember early experiences.
- Can restore some dormant speech and a limited amount of rational thinking. Interact with others, but only in a loving, validating, genuine relationship.
- Cannot play games with rules, are impatient. Want immediate satisfaction of needs.

Stage Four: Vegetation

In vegetation, the old-old person shuts out the world completely, gives up the struggle to resolve living. Self-stimulation is minimal, enough to survive. When the person in Stage Three is tranquilized, restrained or reality oriented, they often retreat to vegetation. The withdrawal is complete.

I have recorded some evidence of response to validation with disoriented old-old in vegetation. Graduate students in 1973 recorded some non verbal responses. One woman's eyes opened and she called her son's name after three months of continual validation.

People in vegetation need touch, recognition and nurturing as long as they live. In helping the disoriented old-old in earlier stages, the worker may prevent movement to the final stage.

Physical Characteristics of Vegetation:
- Eyes are mostly closed, not focused or blank.
- Muscles loose.
- Sit slumped in a chair or lie in bed in a fetal position.
- Have lost awareness of their body.
- Movements are barely perceptible.

Psychological Characteristics of Vegetation:
- Do not recognize close relatives.
- Rarely express feelings of any kind.
- Do not initiate any activity.
- There is no way of knowing if they are resolving.

PART THREE

IMPLEMENTING INDIVIDUAL VALIDATION

Three Steps

Step 1: Gather information

In order to practice Validation, the workers *must* know the person with whom they are working. That means knowing their past, present and future expectations. This assessment also gives the worker a baseline knowledge for evaluating progress. The "Individual Evaluation Progress" form on page 114, and the "History and Baseline Behavior Chart" on page 112, will help you record the information you need to practice Validation, and to evaluate progress after your validation sessions. You will want to learn the following:

- Stage of disorientation.
- Unfinished life tasks, emotions that have not been expressed.
- Unfulfilled basic human needs (see page 71).
- Past relationships i.e.: family, friends, authority figures, death of significant others, children, partner, siblings.
- Jobs, hobbies, unfulfilled ambitions.
- Importance of religion.
- Ways of facing crises.
- How did the person face old age losses?
- Medical history, ask the person directly, read the medical records. Review the psychiatric history for any indication of mental illness in early life.

There are three ways of gathering this information: taking a verbal history, observing the physical characteristics and asking relatives. Because old-old maloriented and disoriented people change, often dramatically throughout the day, the worker must gather information over a period of at least two weeks, meeting with the old person at different times of the day.

History-taking leads to a meaningful relationship. The more you know about a person, the easier it is to use the Validation techniques. You will build trust, which leads to feelings of safety for the disoriented old person. When people feel safe, they gain strength: interactions increase, people begin to speak, they share thoughts and feelings, heightening their self-esteem and sense of dignity. If the person is verbal, ask both "Here and Now" and "There and Then" questions when you take the history. Phrase your questions carefully to avoid raising the old person's anxiety. The maloriented may forget important dates; don't ask questions that refer to specific lengths of time.

"Here and Now" questions:
1. Have you been in this home (hospital, day care center) a long time? (Rather than, "How long have you been in this home?")
2. How do you like the food? The staff? The medical care? Your roommate?
3. Is there enough to do here?
4. Have you been sick since you got here?
5. Are there a lot of activities?
6. What are the other people like? Are they friendly?
7. What brought you here?
8. Are you ever lonely?
9. Is your bed comfortable? Can you sleep at night?
10. Does your roommate make noises at night that disturbs you? What do you do about that?
11. Does it ever bother you when you can't remember a name or a date right away? What do you do then?

The following reactions are typical responses and can help you determine which stage the person is in, most of the time.

The Oriented, integrated old person will usually respond:
V/W: Have you lived here a long time?
Oriented-88-year-old: More than three years. It takes time to get used to the place, but now I like it fine. It's not like my own home,...

If the person is maloriented, they will be aware of the present, but will complain about present day circumstances and will avoid answering questions that refer to feelings:

V/W: Have you lived here a long time?

Maloriented man: Too long. Every minute is too long. This place smells so bad, it's disgusting. They've never heard of deodorants here. But what can you do with these old people. It's a shame.

If the person is verbal but time-confused, they will not respond to Here and Now Questions. They will instead refer to their former home, their parents, siblings, or jobs:

V/W: Have you been here a long time?

85-year-old-time-confused Woman: This is my home. I live here. I take care of my sister. My mother is outside.

The person in repetitive motion will not answer with dictionary words, but will blend sounds to form unique words:

V/W: Have you lived here a long time?

92-year-old-Woman in repetitive motion: The sums of the somms stick to the senses and I can't get them to fit the allfalls.

"There and Then" questions:
1. Have you been sick a lot during your life?
2. What brought you to the home (day care center, etc.)?
3. Before you came here, were you living in your own home or with your family?
4. Were you born in the this country? Was it hard to move?
5. When your wife (husband) got sick, how did you manage? Did your children help?
6. Did you have children? Brothers and sisters?
7. What work did your spouse do? What work did you do?
8. Was your father born in this country? What was his work?
9. Did your mother work?
10. Were you the oldest? The youngest? Did you help take care of your brother(s) or sister(s)?
11. Were your parents strict?
12. What did you do to have fun? Did you like to cook? To dance? Did you sing in Church? Did you go out a lot, or did you like

to stay home?
13. Did you travel to other countries? (Mention specific countries to give alternative choices.)
14. Did you have a good marriage? Was he/she with you when you needed them?
15. What did you do to survive hard times?
16. What was the hardest time in your life? The worst time? The best time?

Questions 4, 5, 10, 11, 14, 15 and 16 refer to coping methods (how a person dealt with difficult situations throughout their life time). Questions 1, 6, 7, 12, 13, 14, 16 explore unfinished life issues.

Often the person may not remember the name of a specific country, or song title. A general question such as, "What song do you like to sing?" can raise anxiety. The more specific a question, the easier it is for the older person to answer. A question that contains the answer gives dignity without anxiety. For example, "Do you like to sing Church songs like, *Jesus Loves Me*, or *Hatikvah*, or *Onward Christian Soldiers*?" "Did you travel to France and Germany?" Phrase the question in a way that the old person can pluck the answer. This shows that you have done your homework, you know and understand the person. The person can trust you. You are nurturing and they feel safe.

If the old person does not remember recent losses and shifts the conversation to their parents and early childhood experiences, he or she is in Stage Two or Three. Denial of all loss signifies Stage One. Clear, vivid images of the distant past with little reference to the present means the person is in Stage Two or Three. People in Stage Four will not respond at all or maintain eye contact with the worker.

Observing the person's physical characteristics is another important way of gathering information. Physical characteristics become a summary of how old people have lived their lives. Wrinkles etched in their faces track their coping methods. An old woman with deep smile lines curving from her nostrils to the corners of her mouth, often smiles to cover anger. Rows of furrows in an old man's forehead, can show a lifetime of worry. An old man with his shoulders hunched to his ears is defending himself from the outside world. Quick, jerky movements from one place to another reflect an inward panic, "Which way should I go? What do I do now?" Wandering, slow, dream-like movements and eyes that are not focused on anything, often mean a retreat to the past.

Begin your non-verbal assessment with the top of the body and carefully work your way down to the feet. Notice their hair. If their hair is carefully combed, either:
- they are oriented and able to perform activities of daily living;
- they are economically able to afford special care;
- they are maloriented and very concerned with maintaining their outward appearance;
- their family visits often and is concerned about their appearance.

If their hair is not combed, it could mean that:
- they are aggressive and no one wants to help them;
- they have poor family relations;
- they can not afford special help;
- they constantly mess up their hair.

Continue down to the face. Look at their eyes. Neurolinguistic Programmers have identified the following physical characteristics and their meanings.[53]

Movement	Meaning
Eyes looking up and to the right	The person is visualizing something
Eyes straight ahead	The person is hearing something
Eyes looking down	The person is feeling something
Rapid breathing	The person is visual
Even breathing	The person is auditory
Deep breathing	The person is kinesthetic
High voice tone	The person is visual
Moderate voice tone	The person is auditory
Low voice tone	The person is kinesthetic

From infancy on, we are developing our preferred sense. See page 41. Of our senses - hearing, seeing, feeling, tasting and smelling - it is the one we use most. In old age, we rely on this preferred sense to create our perception of the world. If this sense is damaged through the natural aging process, we especially suffer. For example: a visual woman who loses her hearing can overcome this loss without a blow to her self-esteem. If she loses her sight, she also loses her main connection to the world, her way of perceiving it is lost.

When you are asking your "here and now", or "there and then" questions, notice the spontaneous eye-movements. If you have just asked, "What was the worst day of your life?" and the person looks up, then you know that most likely he or she is visualizing the scene and is a visual person. You will build trust by using visual words. See the sections on *Techniques* for specific applications of the preferred sense.

Look at the lower lip, the cheeks, the position of the chin, changes in skin color, shoulders, arms, hands, fingers, chest, legs, and feet. Observe the person's movement in space, even if they use a walker or a wheelchair. Don't come to any conclusions at this point. Record your observations throughout the two week period of gathering information.

Step 2: Assess the Stage of Disorientation

Match your observations of physical characteristics and your information from the verbal history with the typical physical and psychological characteristics of the four stages of disorientation, listed in the Part Two. Remember, people change throughout the day. Knowing the stage will help you choose the appropriate Validation techniques to use.

Step 3: Meet with the Person Regularly, Use Validation Techniques.

Fill out the "Individual Validation Treatment Plan" (page 110). The length of time that one works with an individual (contact time) depends upon the person's verbal capacity, attention span, and the amount of time that a worker has available. With maloriented people, contact time should be between 5 and 15 minutes. Contact with Stage Two can be between 2 and 10 minutes. Contact time with Stages Three and Four should be limited to 1-10 minutes. It's quality, not quantity time, that counts. If the worker is available, and the person receptive, use more time. If the old person is in a long-term care facility, interactions should take place at least three times a week; more frequently, for example three times a day, if the person is in an acute-care facility. Interactions can be less frequent if you are working with someone in an out-patient situation, such as at home or in a day-care center. No matter how frequently or infrequently you meet, you must always come back when you have said you would.

Close the interview/interaction when you see any one of the following visible signs of anxiety reduction: with a person in Stage One, the voice is less harsh; the breathing is even; the pulse is normal; the pupils are no longer dilated; the lower lip is relaxed; or the person is smiling. With a person in Stage Two, after you have achieved a moment of intimacy; the person responds with words; speech improves; their gait improves; after you have helped the person to interact with others and they no longer need you. With a person in Stage Three, the repetitive behavior decreases; you have made intimate contact; the negative acting out turns to music, movement or some other form of expression that meets their needs. With persons in Stage Four, after three minutes regardless of the reaction.

Validation can take place anywhere. The housekeeper in a nursing home can validate while she's tidying the room; the nursing assistant, while she is taking the old person to the toilet; the nurse, as she's giving medication; the electrician, while he's changing the light bulbs; the gardener while he's mowing the grass; the family member while he or she is visiting. The only consideration is privacy. This must be a one-to-one relationship that is built on trust, created in a private environment. It can take place in a large room with other people, but you must create an intimate space, safe from critical comments or anxiety provoking intrusions.

In all cases, the Validation worker must:
- be centered (see page 42).
- observe physical characteristics (eyes, muscles, chin, voice-tone, movement, etc.).
- listen with energy.
- not argue the "truth" of facts.
- not be judgmental.
- be aware of each person's private space, both physically and psychologically.

The following techniques are ways to begin a relationship. There is no single formula because every person is different. Each worker must tap his ability to empathize with disoriented old-old. The worker who is honest, genuine, and caring cannot hurt the disoriented old-old person. The wise old person will forgive you if you make a mistake.

Techniques for Stage One, Malorientation:

1. Center yourself. (See page 42) Maloriented people are often hurtful and mean. They turn away friends and family. The Validation worker acknowledges the hurt, puts it in the closet, and tunes into the world of the maloriented. Later, you can express your feelings in your Validation team meeting. (See page 98 on Teams.)

2. Use "who, what, where, when, how" questions to explore. Be a reporter. Explore facts. Avoid feelings. Validate feelings only when the person expresses them. Never ask "why", maloriented people won't know why and it asks for an intellectual answer.

3. Rephrase. Repeat the gist of what the person has said using their key words, i.e. the words that they emphasize or accentuate by changing pitch, which indicates an emotional undertone.

4. Use their preferred sense. Visual words: notice, imagine, picture, remind. Hearing words: hear, listen, loud, sounds like, clear. Kinesthetic words and phrases: feels like, sense, I'm in touch with, that grabs me, strikes me, hits me, that hurts.

5. Use polarity, ask the extreme:
    Resident: They steal my underwear.
    Worker: How often? How much do they take?

    Resident: It hurts.
    Worker: How bad is the pain? When is it the worst?

6. Help the person imagine what would happen if the opposite were true.
Resident: They poison my food.
Worker: Is there any time that they don't poison it.

Resident: There's a man under my bed.
Worker: Is there any time that he's not there?

7. Reminiscing. Exploring the past can re-establish familiar coping methods which the person can use to survive present day crises. Words like "always" and "never" can trigger early memories.
Resident: I can't sleep at night.
Worker: Did this always happen? Did you have this problem when you lived with your husband?

People in Stage One retreat from close, intimate relationships and are threatened by feelings. A handshake, a gentle touch on the forearm is enough intimacy for the maloriented. Hugs are often embarrassing and too close for comfort. Tune into the person's need for touch, not your own. Be aware of their need to defend themselves, however, once intimacy is established, some maloriented people want to be touched. Follow their lead.

Before you leave, honestly express your caring and give the maloriented person a respectful handshake. Leave when their anxiety is reduced: breathing is even, voice is level, muscles are relaxed and the eyes are calm (between 5 and 15 minutes of Validation.) Remember that many fear rejection. Say when you are coming back and return on time. If you have been working with someone within a facility and are leaving the facility, ask a team member to replace you. Maloriented people do not form new relationships easily; give them at least two weeks to grieve, reminisce and help them to relate to your replacement.

Example of Validation with Stage One

Characters:	Mr. Frank, age 96, a new resident in a nursing home
	Worker, age 52, a nurse trained in Validation
Place:	the nursing station

Time: 10:30 a.m., prime time for high energy, ability to think clearly

Goal: Build a trusting relationship. Help Mr. Frank survive the crisis of leaving the community to come live in a nursing home. Help him in his struggle to express bottled up anger and hurt.

Medical: Mr. Frank had a slight stroke 10 years ago. He suffers from Paget's Disease of the knee. He recently had a prostate operation. He has poor vision, otherwise he's in good physical condition. His psychiatric diagnosis is: "SDAT" (Senile Dementia of the Alzheimer's Type) with paranoid delusions.

Social: His niece reports that: Mr.Frank's parents were very strict; he was divorced; has no close friends; his father told him he was "no good" and he didn't do well at school as a child. He made a fair living as a tailor. His hobby is walking. After his prostate operation he blamed the surgeon for castrating him and he seems angry at all authority.

Worker's Observation of Physical Characteristics:
He sits stiffly, his jaw juts out, eyes are narrowed, cheek muscles and lower lip are tight, breathing is deep. His hands clutch his cane as if to protect himself and will not let anyone take it, even when he is eating. He speaks in a low, harsh, accusing voice. When asked a direct question he looks down. The veins in his neck protrude when he is angry. His movements in space are quick, tight, jerky and direct.

Evaluation: There are signs of Stage One: denial, blaming, occasional disorientation. His repeated expression of rage at male authorities indicates his need to resolve angry feelings that have been bottled up. His cane seems to represent potency. His preferred sense is kinesthetic. His unfinished life task is rebellion. Because he has never achieved intimacy with anyone, it will be difficult to establish trust. He needs structured, consistent Validation, for 10 to 15 minutes at least once each day.

Validation Interaction:
> The worker does not threaten Mr. Frank with feeling words. She uses a respectful matter-of-fact voice-tone, shakes hands and stays outside Mr. Frank's 20 inch private space. She meets his eyes only for a moment and does not probe with words or eyes. She calls Mr. Frank by his last name, in respect to his age and experience. She never looks down on him, but sits next to him on an equal plane. She never argues, even though his facts are often "wrong".

Mr.F	That no good goddamn phony. The Herr Doktor.(He spits on the floor in disgust.)
Worker	Who is the Herr Doktor? (Technique 2)
Mr.F	That s.o.b. hates me. He put manure in my room to make me fall. Dumped garbage all over. Then tore all the pages out of my calendar so I don't even know what holiday is coming up. I can't stand it anymore.
Worker	He's driving you crazy? (Technique 4, kinesthetic)
Mr.F	He does it on purpose.
Worker	You mean he deliberately wants to get you? (Technique 3)
Mr.F	That's right!
Worker	Does he do it every day? (Technique 5)
Mr.F	Not only during the day, but at night. Night's are the worst. He doesn't let me sleep. He gives me a roommate who snores and flushes the toilet all the time.
Worker	(technique 1 - don't laugh) Is there any time when you *can* sleep through the night?
Mr.F	When you're on night duty. But that's only once a month.
Worker	Was it always this way? (Technique 7)
Mr.F	When I lived with my niece I could sleep. You remind me of her. She always read me from the bible for a few minutes. And then I could sleep.
Worker	Do you have a bible?

The worker now has a trusting relationship with Mr. Frank because she wasn't confrontational and stepped into his world. She helped him find his own solution to his sleeping problem and helped him to express his anger at authority. After six weeks of one-to-one Validation, for 10 minutes a day, change will occur. The anger will lessen as he expresses it. The worker needs only to listen and not judge. He will remain in Stage One with constant validation and not retreat into Stage Two. He will never stop blaming, however. He is always resolving his unfinished life tasks, they will never be resolved. The more adequate he feels, the less he needs to blame the authority, because he no longer feels like a victim.

Techniques for Stage Two: Time Confusion

1. Center.

2. Use "who, what, where, when, how" questions - never "why".

3. Re-phrase.

4. Use the preferred sense.

5. Polarity, ask the extreme.

6. Touch. Move close into the invisible circle that protects us all. Stage Two persons need nurturing and close body contact. They need the stimulus of another human being to reawaken sleeping nerve cells. They have significant loss of vision and hearing and therefore need to be close in order to see and hear another person. Approach the person directly from the front. Approaching from the side may startle them because people in Stage Two have usually lost the ability to see out of the corner of the eye (peripheral vision).

7. Use genuine, direct, prolonged eye contact. Touch with your eyes. Bend or sit down if the person is in a wheelchair in order to make direct eye contact.

8. Use a clear, low, warm, loving voice tone. Harsh tones cause withdrawal or anger. High, weak, soft tones are ignored due to damage to the auditory nerve. Use your diaphragm to project a nurturing clear voice. The voice triggers memories of loved

ones. Speak while making eye contact and touching the person in Stage Two, they need the combined stimuli of touch, eye contact and voice in order to respond. Do not speak without touching. Avoid speaking to the person's back, this may raise fear of the unknown.

9. <u>Observe the emotion</u>. Stage Two persons freely express their feelings. Words begin to fail. The worker must now communicate on an emotional, rather than on a verbal level. A discrete observation of the physical characteristics leads to an objective assessment of the emotion.

10. <u>Match their emotion</u> with your face, body, breathing and voice tone. You can recall the feeling within yourself by thinking of a time in your life when you felt the same way. There are only four, raw, human emotions, which all of us have experienced with varying degrees of intensity:
    love/pleasure/joy/sex
    anger/rage/hate/displeasure
    fear/guilt/shame/anxiety
    sadness/misery/grief

11. <u>Express their emotion, with emotion.</u>
    A woman is walking frantically out the door saying, "My mother needs me." She is looking up, away from the worker. Her breathing is labored and deep. Her lower lip is pursed. Her shoulders are hunched. Her fingers are clenched. She shuffles towards the door.
    Worker, "You're worried. Is your mother alone?"

12. <u>Ambiguity.</u> Use "he", "she", "it", "they", "something", or "someone." When people can no longer use dictionary words and you don't understand what they are trying to say, use vague pronouns to substitute for words that you don't understand. You don't need to know the meaning of each word.
    Resident, "Flu Flu didn't come home."
    Worker, "Do you think something happened to him?"

13. <u>Link the behavior to the need.</u> There are three basic human needs:
    to be safe/secure/loved
    to be useful/working/active
    to express raw emotions and to be heard
    A man who was a farmer is looking out the window anxiously and then at the clock. He says, "I have to go home." Worker, "Do your cows need milking?" She acknowledges his need to be useful.

14. <u>Use music.</u> Familiar songs, learned in childhood and repeated throughout life, become permanently imprinted in their memory. When the V/W sings a well-remembered melody, the time-confused relate immediately.

Example of Validation with Stage Two

Characters: Mrs. Gate, age 96
            Her daughter, age 52, trained in Validation
Place: The daughter's home
Time: 2:00 a.m.

Mrs. G.   (pulling clothes out of her drawers) It's not here. The noodles are tangled. No room in this tomb.
Daughter (touches her mother's arm, looks at her eyes and says in a low, nurturing tone) Noodles? (Techniques 3, 6, 7, 8)
Mrs. G.   My noodles are tangled (points to her head). Get Daddy. Get Daddy.
Daughter You mean your brain is tangled? You feel mixed up in your noodle? (Technique 13)
Mrs. G.   Yes. Yes (looks relieved). Daddy can fix my noodle.
Daughter Daddy always straightened your noodle. You miss Daddy a lot. Were you looking for him just now (points to the drawer)? (Technique 11, 13)
Mrs. G.   He's not here. Nowhere. He left the punts.
Daughter He left it? (Technique 12) And you were all alone?
Mrs. G.   All alone.
Daughter (touching her on the back of her head with her finger tips in a circular motion) When Daddy was with you, you

were never alone? You feel alone now. (Technique 6, 11)

Mrs. G. (smiles at her daughter)

Daughter (sings *Take me out to the ball game*, a song her father frequently sang)

Mrs. G. (sings along, remembering every word)

Mrs. Gate uses vivid images, sharing her feelings of love with her daughter. The genuine caring of the daughter triggers feelings of comfort. One moment of clock-time becomes 50 years of feeling-time.

The daughter continues talking with her mother as she helps her return to bed. She never lies by telling her mother that "Daddy is still alive" nor does she press the facts by saying, "Daddy is dead." Her mother chose to forget that her husband has died. She needs to restore him in order to survive loneliness. Deep down, on the same subliminal level in which a sleeper brushes away a fly, Mrs. Gate *knows* that her husband is dead.[54] If the daughter had pointed out that painful fact, Mrs. Gate would have withdrawn or become angry. The daughter has replaced Daddy as a symbol of love and security.

The daughter should use Validation for no more than 5 to 10 minutes whenever her mother becomes time-confused. The relationship remains intact, the mother keeps communicating with dictionary words, and does not regress to repetitive motion.

Techniques for Stage Three: Repetitive Motion

Techniques 2-5 are verbal, and are only used if, and when the Stage Three person relates on a verbal level.

1. Center.

2. Use "who, what, where, when, how" questions - never "why."

3. Re-phrase.

4. Use the preferred sense.

5. <u>Polarity</u>, ask the extreme.

6. <u>You must begin with touching.</u> Where you touch the person is important. Because early, emotionally-tinged memories are permanently imprinted in the brain's circuits, the V/W can kindle a significant relationship by touching Stage Three persons in the same way that they were touched by a loved one in childhood. After 30 years of practice I have found the following:

   - Using the palm of the hand, in a light circular motion on the upper cheek stimulates feelings of "being mothered", a mother relationship, a familiar "rooting" reflex.
   - Using the finger tips, in a circular motion, medium pressure, on the back of the head, stimulates feelings of "being fathered", a father relationship, being patted on the head as a small child.
   - Using the outside of the hand, placing the little finger under the ear lobe, curving along the chin, with both hands, a soft stroking motion downward along the jaw, stimulates feelings of having a "spouse/lover", a sexual relationship.
   - Using cupped fingers on the back of the neck, with both hands, in a small circular motion, stimulates feelings of "motherhood or fatherhood", touching a child.
   - Using the full hand on the shoulders and upper back by the shoulder blades, with full pressure, in a rubbing movement, stimulates feelings of "being a sibling or good friend", a brother or sister relationship.
   - Touching with the finger tips on the inside of the calf stimulates feelings of caring for animals, such as horses and cows.

7. <u>Use genuine, direct, prolonged eye contact.</u>

8. <u>Use a clear, low, nurturing voice tone.</u>

9. <u>Observe the emotion.</u>

10. <u>Match their emotion.</u>

11. <u>Say their emotion, with emotion.</u>

12. <u>Use ambiguity</u>, the vague pronoun.

13. <u>Link the behavior to the need</u>. In this stage the need for love is often expressed by folding, rocking, or pursing the lips to make a clucking sound. The need to feel useful is expressed by moving familiar muscles that were used in working. The need to express raw emotion is expressed by shouting, swearing, pounding, or crying. Please refer to the list of symbols that are on pages 46 and 48, they are particularly important when people act out rather than verbalize.

14. <u>Use music</u>. When people don't use speech, the V/W can communicate through singing familiar songs, prayers, familiar, early-learned poems and nursery rhymes.

15. <u>Mirroring</u>. Copy the body movements, breathing, look in the eye, position of the lower lip, hand and feet movements, and any vocalizations. This must be done without judgement, self-consciousness, or patronizing. This is not a game; people in Stage Three are not children. You are trying to understand the reason behind their behavior, in order to link the behavior to the need: love, identity, or expression of feelings.

Example: a man is sitting in a wheelchair, repeatedly pounding his fist into his other, open hand. The V/W approaches him from the front, stoops down to his eye level or lower, and begins to pound her fist into her other hand using the same rhythm and intensity. She picks up his way of breathing (rapid, shallow, or deep), the look on his face and in his eyes. After 30 seconds, the man stops pounding and looks at her. She also stops pounding. There are five seconds of silent eye contact. The worker says, "You're working hard." The man answers, "Damn right."

The Validation Apron was developed particularly for Stage Three people by Isabelle Vardon and Everett Smith, M.D. It is an apron that has various attachments held on with velcro, that the elderly person can work with throughout the day. Each apron is created with the individuals' needs in mind. For instance, a former waitress would have a pocket filled with napkins for her to fold; a former banker would have a folder filled with play money for him to count; a former secretary would have a pad and pen.**

Example of Validation with Stage Three:

Characters: Mrs. Mint, age 93
           Geriatric nursing assistant, age 22, trained in Validation
Place: The nursing home bathroom. Mrs. Mint is walking back and forth anxiously.
Time: 10:00 p.m.

Mrs. M.   (tears streaming down her cheeks) Fetzlet. Fetzlet. (She looks under the toilet, the sink, the cabinet.)
V/W   (matching Mrs. M.'s breathing, voice tone, her hand and feet movements) They're gone? You can't find them? (Technique 9, 10, 12, 15)
Mrs. M.   All gone. I fudet it and it fitzed. (Her crying increases.)
V/W   (touching Mrs. M. on the back of her neck gently) You miss it so much. (The worker's voice reflects Mrs. M.'s loneliness and despair.) (Technique 6, 10, 11, 12, 13)
Mrs. M.   (stops moving and looks at the worker, grieving)
V/W   (holds the eye contact for ten seconds, matching the grief in Mrs. M.'s eyes, puts her arms around Mrs. M. gently stroking the back of her neck and shoulders, begins to sing) *Jesus loves me...* (Technique 7, 9, 10, 15)
Mrs. M.   (sings the entire song with the worker. She weeps, then stops crying, smiles at the worker and strokes her hair.) What a nice girl.

Mrs. Mint never cried when her third child died of pneumonia. Her daughter reports that her mother rarely expressed her emotions. In

---

** The Validation apron is available from Vardon and Smith at: Northwood Care Inc., 2615 Northwood Terrace, Halifax, Nova Scotia, B3K 3S5 Canada her old age, Mrs. Mint is healing herself by crying for her lost child. Now in Stage Three disorientation she needs someone to listen as she releases her grief for the first time.

It's hard to let someone stand there and cry, and have the crying get worse. The worker is not hurting the old person by letting them cry. What hurts is allowing the feelings to remain strangled inside. The worker is helping Mrs. Mint make peace. Expression and validation of feelings, will relieve them. At the end, the worker is becoming a substitute for Mrs. Mint's child.

Techniques for Stage Four: Vegetation

1. Center.

2. Touch.

3. You can try getting eye contact, but it's very difficult. If you can get eye contact, you have succeeded.

4. Use a genuine, nurturing voice tone.

5. Use ambiguity.

6. Link the behavior to the need.

7. Use music.

It is very important to know the social history of a person in the Vegetation stage because you have noting else to go on. The person gives no emotional "affect". There are no outside clues to what is going on inside them. We trust, however, that there is something going on inside them. The Validation goals for Stage Four are to get:

* eye contact
* facial movement
* some type of emotional response: singing, smiling, crying
* some kind of physical movement: hands, feet

Example of Validation with Stage Four:

Characters: Mr. Simons, age 88
                The physical therapist, age 32
Place: In Mr. S.'s room, he is in bed and has a feeding tube.
Time: 10:30 a.m.

Mr. Simons is lying in bed, eyes closed, his breathing is slow and labored. He makes no body movements. His eyes flicker every once and awhile. The worker gently rubs his calf muscles knowing that he was a rancher. She sings *Home, Home on the Range.* Mr. Simons' eyelids flicker, but he does not open his eyes. His lower lip curves upward slightly. The worker sings for one more minute and then leaves. She returns three hours later and repeats the rubbing and singing. Mr. Simons opens his eyes. The worker bends down for eye contact and moves close so that Mr. Simons can see her singing. She now touches his cheek gently with the palm of her hand and continues the song. Mr. Simons keeps his eyes open during the song and closes them when she stops. She leaves.

This one-to-one validation should be applied six times a day, for one minute, as long as the person lives. It is best done by a Validation team.

Typical Mistakes and Reactions:

This section is to reassure you that even when you feel that you have made a mistake, it can be corrected. Remember, old people are wise, they will forgive your mistakes.

Mistake: You mistake a Stage One person for Stage Two and begin to talk about emotional issues with a maloriented person.
Reaction: "Don't you have other things to do?" The person will push you and the topic away, maybe getting angry.
Correction: Use "who, what, where, when, how." Say, "What do you think I should be doing?" This will help change the subject and salvage the relationship.

Mistake: Touching someone who doesn't want to be touched.

Reaction: The person flinches and draws back, when you touch him. *Correction*: Know that you are working with a maloriented person who is afraid of intimacy. Use polarity and say, "What bothers you the most about people who butt into your business?" Or, verbalize the behavior, "You are an independent person, aren't you?"

Mistake: Not touching someone who needs to be touched. *Reaction*: The person doesn't respond to your verbal exploring. *Correction*: Touch them in the appropriate way for Stage Two or Three. Or if you have been touching them, touch them in a different place; they may not be feeling your touch due to poor circulation.

Mistake: Using a soft, childlike, or harsh voice tone. *Reaction*: None, or rejecting. *Correction*: Think of someone you love, so that your voice becomes nurturing, adult and reassuring. Check that you're talking loud enough for them to hear you.

Mistake: Positioning yourself outside of the person's range of vision. *Reaction*: The person doesn't respond, or continues repetitive pounding, pacing, or crying out. *Correction*: Realize that they don't see you. Move in closer and directly in front of the person. Frequently old-old people have no peripheral vision.

Mistake: Your body movements don't match what you are saying. When a person is trying to leave the building you ask, "Do you have to see your mother?" while at the same time you are curling your fingers around their arm in a restraining way. *Reaction*: The person continues to try to leave or shakes you off. *Correction*: Acknowledge your own need to restrain them so that they will stay. Put your own needs away and tune into those of the old-old person. Mirror the person's way of walking, pick up their breathing rhythms, the look in their eyes and say the emotion that you see out loud.

Mistake: You see a person who is acting out their anger or grief and ask them, "You seem angry (sad). Let's talk about it." *Reaction*: The person ignores you.

Correction: Stop being a therapist, the person doesn't want to be analyzed. Mirror and match their emotion. Use your feelings more. If they can't talk, verbalize their emotions through a song that matches their feelings.

Mistake: Using words that don't match the preferred sense. An old woman says, "That man is making noises all night long." You answer, "What does he look like?"
Reaction: "I don't know, I didn't see him." It is harder for the person to respond to your questions.
Correction: Say, "How loud were the noises? What did it sound like? Was it a banging?"

Mistake: Patronizing the person. A woman says, "I have to see my mother, she's very sick." You answer, "The doctor is there, they're giving her medicine and she'll be fine."
Reaction: "No, No, No. I have to see her right now. She needs me."
Correction: Mirror the emotion and rephrase what she has said using the preferred sense. "You're worried about your mother. Is she very pale?"

Mistake: Well intentioned lying. An old woman says, "I see a man under my bed." You answer, "Isn't he good looking."
Reaction: Withdrawal. Deep down on a subliminal level, the woman knows that there isn't any man under the bed and that you are patronizing.
Correction: Say, "What does he look like?" and move on to other verbal Validation techniques.

Mistake: Trying to analyze or give insight. The resident says, "The one in the kitchen is poisoning my food." You answer, "Does she remind you of your mother?" trying to make the person realize that they are projecting feelings about their mother onto the cook. You have obtained this information from her daughter.
Reaction: "My mother was a wonderful cook! I wish you could have tasted her food."
Correction: Use a different verbal technique. Example: "What does the food taste like? Which meal is the worst, breakfast or lunch?"

Mistake: You don't come back when you say you will.
Reaction: The resident says to another worker, "You can't trust her, she told me she'd be here at 3:30 and now it's 3:50 and she's not here."
Correction: When you return say: "It's a terrible thing to be late. I'm sorry I was late. What did you think happened when I didn't come? Did that ever happen before?"

Mistake: You are afraid you're going to uncover something horrible that has been hidden, so you don't explore or touch. The person is crying, and you say, "It's OK. Everything is going to be all right."
Reaction: The person either continues crying and doesn't respond to you at all, or they stop expressing their feelings to please you.
Correction: Say, "You were/are crying. Is it very bad?" Trust that very old people will protect themselves and not let you bring up something that they don't want to face.

Mistake: You have worked for a long time with a maloriented person who said there was a drip from the ceiling that wet her bed. The behavior stopped and you stopped visiting her. A year later, after her daughter moved 3000 miles away, the woman again complains about the drip from the ceiling. The mistake is that you stopped visiting her. Even though she didn't need Validation, she needed your relationship. When her daughter left, it triggered an earlier memory of when she lost her controls i.e. became incontinent. The present day fear of losing her child, is the same as the fear of losing control of her bladder. The facts are different, the fears are the same.
Correction: Come back and begin Validation again, this time don't cut off contact when or if, the drip goes away.

PART FOUR

VALIDATION GROUPS

Seven Steps

The basic principle of group work is to provide a safe environment where people learn to trust each other, so that they can:
- express their feelings
- interact with each other verbally and non-verbally
- solve common problems
- perform social roles
- learn controls
- achieve a sense of worth

This principal holds true for all small groups, as well as for Validation groups.[55]

A Validation group worker:
- provides a physically safe place to meet, with privacy.
- provides a psychologically safe place, where people will not hurt one another.
- facilitates interaction between group members.
- states simply, using one-syllable words, and sentences without clauses, two alternatives to a problem.
- establishes a ritual, a structured beginning, middle and end.
- gives familiar social roles to each group member, that restore dignity and do not raise anxiety.
- evaluates progress.
- coordinates staff support and the necessary materials for each group meeting (program media).

The goals of a Validation group are to stimulate:
- energy.
- social roles.
- identity.
- interaction.
- verbal behaviors.
- social controls.

- well-being and happiness.

A group should also:
- reduce anxiety.
- prevent vegetation.
- reduce the need for tranquilizers and restraints.
- reduce burn out in the staff and in families.

A group works well with people who are time-confused and those who are in repetitive motion. People in Stage Two and Three have little energy or attention span for one-on-one conversations. In a group, people look at each other, sit close, touch each other through dancing and hand-holding. Energy spreads. Groups trigger memories of family roles, of former social group roles and of social controls. People begin to listen and their speech improves. They begin to care about others in the group, modeling the nurturing worker. By sharing common problems, they solve each other's conflicts. They regain dignity through increased control over their lives. They validate each other.

Maloriented persons who are afraid of feelings and cannot face their recent memory loss, do not belong in a Validation group. The worker would have to limit the maloriented, who often whine, complain, or blame other group members for their own failures. Only after a successful one-to-one relationship, can a maloriented person join a group. Maloriented persons can benefit from a reality-based group that does not stress immediate recall of the present day or date; a group that reviews current events; a Resident's Council that recommends changes in management of the facility; a task-oriented group, such as baking, cooking, or flower-arranging; a Remotivation group; or a Reminiscing group that does not dwell on emotions. (See page 96 for a description of Remotivation, Reminiscing and Reality Orientation groups.) A maloriented person can become the worker's assistant in the Validation group, but not a group member.

Step 1: Gather information

Assess the stage of disorientation just as you would when working with individuals. Observe the physical and psychological characteristics of the potential group members. Use questions that explore the past. Know the people well. Use the questionnaire *Selecting Members for Validation Groups*, on page 113, and the *Individual Validation Treatment Plan*, on page 110. The success of your group will depend heavily on how well you know each person.

Step 2: Select Members

In order to select members, you need to know the following about each person:
- What social role would they be comfortable with? A former preacher could be the prayer leader, a former housewife could be the hostess, a former church choir singer could be the song leader.
- What is your goal for this individual? Be specific, for example: less crying, improved gait, makes eye contact with others, more speech, etc.
- What stage is the person in <u>most</u> of the time?
- What topic, or unresolved issue will engage this person: unexpressed grief over the death of a child? an unhappy marriage? loss of a spouse?
- What music do they respond to? Were they active in a church choir, a barber shop quartet, etc?
- What is their capacity for movement? Can they bear weight? You need to know the medical history.
- What is their potential for relationships with other members? Where should they sit? A woman who misses her husband should sit next to a man who misses his wife; an early onset Alzheimer's person should sit next to a nurturing parent type.

Use the questionnaire on page 113, *Selecting Member for Validation Groups*. Select five to ten people in Stages Two and Three. You should have the following:
- one Stage Two person with leadership ability (head of a volunteer group, a "club" person, a business person).
- a person with wise, motherly qualities in Stage Two.
- four to five Stage Two people who like to talk. You can include early onset Alzheimer's patients who's behavior can

be predicted and who will not strike others.
- no more than two Stage Three persons. Choose people in Stage Three who respond immediately to the worker's touch. Constant, repetitive motion can destroy the meeting, creating anxiety for the entire group.
- maloriented people who can help the worker, for example, as a violin player.

Do not include:
- Stage Three people who will not sit down, or cannot stop loud, constant, repetitive motions in the group.
- severe early on-set Alzheimer's patients, in the last stages, whose behaviors you can not predict. See the section on Alzheimer's Disease, page 30.
- maloriented people or oriented people. They will be afraid or angry and disruptive to the meeting.
- aphasic elderly who are oriented to present day reality.
- mentally ill elderly, whose behavior you can not predict.
- retarded elderly who are oriented to present day reality.
- chronically ill old people whose illness is not related to the aging process.

Step 3: Find Roles for Each Member

Roles give structure to the meetings and help each individual to participate. The Welcomer opens and closes the meeting, the Hostess serves the refreshments, the Song Leader leads the group in singing, etc. Roles ought to make the group members feel useful and necessary to the group; roles ought to stimulate old patterns of behavior and feelings of self-worth.

The worker assigns roles that match the background of each individual. Do not continue roles that cause anxiety. A former secretary may not want to take minutes of the group meetings, fearful of failure. She can become the Song Leader, if she enjoys singing. Wrongly assigned roles can be corrected and changed as people change. Roles in a Validation group are best assigned when people spontaneously choose to perform them. A person who hums all the time can become the Song Leader. An angry man who tells everyone to "shut up" can become the Opening and Closing Chairman, who limits other members. A kleenex-twister can become the Napkin Passer, etc. The worker watches carefully to match the roles to the individuals and must help them assume their roles.

Do not switch roles once the person has performed well. People need the security of performing the same role at each meeting. With security, comes dignity.

Possible Group Roles:

- Welcomer or Chairperson, the task leader who opens and closes each meeting.
- Song Leader, Rhythm Leader, Bandleader
- Poetry Reader
- Chair Arranger, Flower Arranger
- Secretary
- Emotional Leader, a motherly person who supports Stage Three members when they cry or pound, etc. The emotional leader usually solves whatever problem is being discussed.
- Host or Hostess, to help pass refreshments.

Step 4: Involve the Staff, All Departments

You will need the support of your administration and co-workers in order to have a Validation group. You can do individual Validation on your own, but not a group. You need key staff to help with:

- transporting the group members to and from the meetings.
- reserving a private place and good time to meet on a regular, weekly basis.
- providing refreshments and equipment.
- getting members ready for the meeting, for example: toileting them beforehand, not sedating them before or during the meeting.
- evaluating the progress of each member.
- suggesting new members.
- suggesting topics.
- maintaining a good atmosphere, for example, not allowing group members to be taken out of the meeting.

Examples of how staff can help:

- The housekeeper warns, "Mrs. G. and Mrs. S. fight. Don't put them in one group.

- The beautician says, "Tuesdays are no good to meet. That's the only day I do their hair."
- The dietician adds, "You can't give them ice-cream. They're diabetic. Try Vita-cream."
- The head nurse, "Why don't you add Mrs. P. She's very motherly."
- The social worker, "We have a new admission that would be perfect, he's in Stage Two disorientation."
- The nurse's aide, "Mr. Cane doesn't hit me after the group meeting, when I bath him."

Meet each week with the nursing department. Share Validation with family members of the residents, as well as with volunteers who work in the facility. Sometimes family members will object if they see their parent holding a doll, for example. You need to explain the Validation principles and goals to help them understand that their parent is restoring his or her role as a mother or father and not going through a second childhood.

Step 5: Include Music, Talk, Movement, Food

A Validation group includes music, talk, movement and food. It spends different amounts of time on each activity, depending on the group mood and the verbal ability of the group members on that particular day. Although each meeting is different, the same order of events, or ritual, gives a sense of safety to group members and security for the worker, especially in the beginning of forming a group. The ritual gives a group rhythm. Members look forward to meetings. They express themselves through talk, music, and movement. They end the meeting, looking forward to the next one.

Music:
People in Stage Two and Three cannot talk during the entire meeting. Songs stimulate interaction and blood flow, reduce anxiety, increase thinking capacity, give feelings of well-being and happiness. You should begin and end each group meeting with singing. If possible chose songs that relate to the topic. For example, if you are discussing missing a spouse, sing *Let Me Call You Sweetheart*. The choice of songs should reflect the cultural and religious background

of the people in your group. Consider church songs, folk tunes, and romantic songs that correspond to the tradition of group members, not the background of the younger worker. Current popular music will not involve group members. Examples of songs: *Daisy, You Are My Sunshine, Let Me Call You Sweetheart, The More We Get Together, When Irish Eyes Are Smiling, I Want A Girl,* etc. Group members can accompany the singing with rhythm instruments, such as drums, tambourines, sticks, and finger cymbals. Creating a rhythm band offers additional roles, as well as an opportunity for group members to interact with other residents and staff by playing for them. Songs end the meeting on an up-beat. Always end the meeting with positive feelings.

Talk:
Always have a discussion topic. Stage Two and Three respond best to topics that bring out feelings of love, belonging, fear of separation, anger, struggle for meaning, and identity - the universal feelings.
Suggested topics:
- missing the parent
- missing one's home
- missing one's job
- missing a spouse, sex, intimate love
- fear of being alone
- fear of losing everything
- boredom, loss of identity
- uselessness, need to belong
- struggle to find a reason for life
- anger at uselessness
- anger at rejection, by parents, children, authorities
- love for each other
- childhood pranks
- punishments
- problems with siblings
- friendship
- how to be happy
- what makes someone angry, sad, happy
- getting along with "crazy" people
- what makes someone "crazy"

- what happens in old-old age
- preparing for death
- how to help each other

Movement:
- Toss a large, soft ball, calling members' names as they catch the ball. Do not expect members to remember each other's name. Toss the ball while singing.
- Each person holds the same elastic ribbon, moving the ribbon to the beat of the music. The worker encourages group members to follow each other's movements. "Mrs. S. is moving the ribbon over her ear. What does that remind you of, Mrs. S.?" "I'm hanging out my wash." "Let's all move like Mrs. S."
- Try partner dancing, swaying, wheelchair dancing, simple square-dances and circle dances such as "the hokey pokey". These create joy, heighten energy and increase feelings of well-being, and closeness. People who are in wheelchairs can often stand and sway to music.
- Move scarves to music.
- Toss bean bags.
- Do arts and crafts projects, such as drawing with big crayons, kneading dough or baking. These activities can help the old-old people express their feelings and trigger feelings of self-worth.

Food:
Refreshments provide nurturing, and trigger adult behavior and social roles. In a social atmosphere, people in Stage Three will become motivated to feed themselves, and often this behavior will continue outside of the group. Since the members themselves pass the food, carefully select food that will not spill, choose cookies that are easily eaten, plates that are light, cups that are easy to handle, and fill the glasses half full, so that the hostess will not be embarrassed by spills. What is served depends on the local culture. Juice and cookies are the norm in the United States.

Step 6: Prepare for the Meeting

Before each meeting prepare the following:

- Plan the agenda. Select the songs and music, the topic for discussion, poems, dances, and refreshments.

- Prepare all the necessary materials and the meeting room. Arrange the chairs in a small, close circle. Members cannot see or hear each other in a large circle. Closeness creates energy.

- Prepare a seating chart for the nursing staff to make sure that people sit next to those that they enjoy being near. Make sure that the worker sits next to the deaf person and the person who needs constant touching and support. Sit opposite the verbal person and the group Chairman, so that people on the sides will enter the energy flow.

   Do not use a table. Energy cannot spread around a table. They prevent hearing, seeing, and touching each other. Tables isolate. Use a table only for painting, drawing, or arts and crafts.

Seating Arrangement in a Group:

Natural Leader
■

Dance Leader   Hostess
Stage Two   ■   ■ Stage Two

Discussion Leader   Song Leader
Stage Two   ■   ■ Stage Two

                                      Emotional Leader
Co-worker ■   ■ Stage Two

Pacer   Deaf person
Stage Three ■   ■ Stage Three

■
Validation worker

- See each group member before the meeting to remind them of the meeting. Pick up clues for topics at that time. For example: a person may be angry because her roommate sat in her chair. This anger can be expressed and resolved during the meeting.

- See the nursing staff to see if anything unusual has happened that might influence the course of the meeting.

- When planning the topic relate it to a specific group member. Make the topic a specific problem that the group can solve such as: "Mrs. Jones is crying because she misses her mother. How can we help her, Mrs. Smith." Ask a specific person who you know is verbal and nurturing. Group members will rally round a person with a problem. The worker states the problem clearly and simply and asks group members to help solve that problem. Conflicts are vital for group interaction. Example:

    Worker: I saw Mrs. Fast this morning. She still looks angry because Mrs. Smith sat in her chair. Let's figure out a way to help Mrs. Fast feel better. Mrs. Fast, tell us what happened?

    The worker helps the two women understand each other. The group members give advice. Solving problems leads to feelings of control and self-worth.

- A tense worker cannot tune into disoriented old-old people. In order to be focused, the worker must be relaxed. Relax before and during the meeting. In order to relax:

    - Concentrate on your center of gravity, a spot one inch below the waist.
    - Breathe slowly in through the nose and out through the mouth. Wash the body with your breath.
    - Stop "inner dialogue." Pay attention to your breath. Focus on your "center".
    - Breath and focus on the "center" for a count of eight.

Step 7: The Meeting

Groups must meet at least once a week, at the same time, in the same place. Meetings can last from 20 minutes to one hour, depending upon the group's energy. Each meeting is born anew. The group has four parts, a birth, a life, a closing, and a preparation for the next meeting.

<u>Birth</u>: Creating energy

- Greet each person in the circle. Use last names to tap adult behavior and show respect. (about 5-7 minutes)
- Mention each individual's role as you move around the circle to remind group members of their social roles.
- Use a caring, energetic, clear, low, resonant voice tone so that everyone can hear the others' names.
- Touch each person. Pick up their body-language cues.
- Bend down for eye-to-eye contact.
- Move close to each person. Severely disoriented people need closeness.
- Listen to each person as you travel around the circle. If one wants to "hang on," assure that person that you will come back to them after you greet the others.
- Seating is very important. Make sure that everyone is in their usual chair.
- Ask the leader to rise (giving them status), and welcome the group. You should sit or kneel to help the leader rise.
- Ask the Song Leader to start the opening song. Sing more songs, read poems, or say prayers. Build energy and closeness.

<u>Life</u>: The verbal part of the group, problem solving

- Introduce the discussion topic or conflict. (about 5-7 minutes) Always help group members make choices by offering alternatives. For example, "Should we talk about mothers or fathers?" Do not ask, "What shall we talk about?" Severely disoriented people will not be able to answer an open question.
- Do not tell group members what to do, but instead present

problems for the group to solve. Trust that the group is wise! Ask the Emotional Leader to solve the problem. The Emotional Leader supports other members, offers reasons for their behavior, welcomes the group, bids them goodbye, expresses feelings for the group, and shows concern. The Emotional Leader should be a wise, nurturing old-old person, with a capacity to share wisdom.

- After the problem has been solved by the group, summarize the interactions. "Mrs. Jones you were so helpful when Mrs. Smith cried. You put your arm around her just when she needed it." "Mr. Jones, without your singing we never would have gotten our group started."
- Use movement. Get people up, if they can stand. A co-worker can dance with the people in wheelchairs. Movement often stimulates verbal ability. You can also do arts and crafts at this time such as: finger painting, mixing dough, planting, working with clay. (about 5-10 minutes)

Closing: Create an upbeat, intimate "we" feeling

- Do your closing ritual. (about 5 minutes) The Song Leader leads the closing song. The Welcomer or Chairman closes the meeting.
- The Hostess or Host can now serve refreshments. (10 minutes) People in Stage Two and Three relate freely in a non-verbal party mood. Meetings should always end on an up-swing, even if the group has discussed angry or sad feelings.
- Say goodbye to each member and that you are looking forward to seeing them at the next meeting.
- The nursing staff can now help with transporting the members back to their floors. It is important to move members into social situations where there is an on-going activity, such as a day room or dining room. If members are isolated after the meeting, they will feel a greater sense of loss and often will start to yell or exhibit other negative behavior. They feel abandoned after having been a part of a warm, social group.

Preparation for the next meeting:

- After each meeting, fill out the *Validation Group Summary Form* on page 115, and the *Evaluation of Progress Form* on page 114. It is important to track the progress of your group for yourself as well as the rest of the staff. Share this information in staff meetings and with patients' family members.

- In between meetings, continue with individual Validation and informal Validation groups on the floor. Nursing staff on all shifts appreciate specific prescriptions for residents. For example:

  Name: Sadie Ford
  Prescription: Fold napkins 3x per day with a nurse's aide

  Names: Mrs. Feld, Mrs. Thomas, Mrs. Field
  Prescription: Sing *Daisy, Daisy*, and/or *You Are My Sunshine* 2x per day, with a nurse's aide who enjoys singing, sitting in a close circle.

How to handle difficult members in the group:
When a member yells, pounds, cries, or exhibits other disruptive behavior, stop the ritual and ask the group to solve the problem.

Worker   Mr. X. is pounding so hard we can't hear each other. (looking at the Emotional Leader) Mrs. S., do you think he's angry at his children?
Leader   Yes. That's what it is. They hurt his feelings.
Worker   Would you ask him?
         (Mr. X. stops pounding as Mrs. S. approaches him. The group continues to help him free his anger. They end the meeting by singing *The More We Get Together*.)

The group gains cohesion and togetherness by solving a problem. If Mr. X. cannot stop pounding, the group can decide to ask the nurse's aide to help him to his room. The group must continue its life. Each meeting presents a problem that the group can solve.

Example of a Validation Group

The worker greets each person in the circle.

Leader Welcome to the Tuesday group. Now shape up! No monkey business today.

Song Leader "Daisy, Daisy...I'm all crazy."

Mr. T. That's right, lady. You are crazy.

Mrs. G. I have to go home. Where are my rubbers. Where is my purse. Help!!!

Mr. T. You're crazy too, lady. You're all crazy!

Worker (stroking Mrs. G.'s arm) I guess we can't sing together because Mr. T feels everyone is crazy. What makes a person crazy?

Mrs. G. Having nothing to do. Get me my rubbers. I have to go to work. The company will pay the fare.

Worker You miss the company, don't you, Mrs. G. Was it a big company?

Mrs. G. Middle size. A Fendall company. Like the symofile curtains. (She points to the curtains.)

Worker How do you mean, symo-file?

Mrs. G. I file everything in the company. (She pats her purse and stuffs napkins in each compartment.)

Worker (patting the purse with Mrs. G.) You are acting like a very efficient file clerk.

Mr. T. She's crazy. That's what she is.

Worker (filing with Mrs. G.) Mr. T., Mrs. G. was a file clerk. Is it crazy to want to do the job you did all your life?

Mrs. G. I am a filer, like Feil here. (The worker's name is Feil and is pronounced like file.)

Worker You mean the files in your company are similar to filing here in this company? In my Feil company?

Mrs. G. That's right. Simo-file. Feil. File. File.

Worker And my name is Feil. File. Feil. You combined the words.

Mrs. G. (smiles and nods)

Worker That sounds nice, symo-file, and Fendall. What is Fendall?

Mrs. G. Memorable friends from the past. The company.

Mr. T. I'll heck her with my pecker. Pecker. Pecker. Pecker. Wanna see the heck-pecker, lady? (He unzips his pants.)

Worker Mr. T., you are unzipping your pants. Do you miss your wife?

Mr. T. You bet your ass. (He stops unzipping his pants.)

Worker (to the Emotional Leader) Mrs. H., what do you do when you miss your husband?

Mrs. H.   I put his picture in the breadbox, so I could talk to him every morning.

Miss J.   Harry, Harry, Harry, Harry. I miss Harry.

Worker   Was Harry your lover, Miss J.?

Mr. T.   Harry's honest as the day is long. His pecker is long. In Detroit Michigan. Honest as his pecker. My wife is a bitch. A bitch, lady.

Worker   Did your wife make you angry? What did she do?

Mr. T.   She is a wooden doll. A doll of wood. She makes coffins. I died last year a thousand deaths.

Worker   She's a doll of wood and she made you die and still you miss her. Miss J., you miss Harry, whom you loved. Mrs. G., you miss the company which you love, and the companions in the company. What can we do to help each other feel better here in this group, with each other?

Miss J.   We can help each other.

Worker   Can we get closer by holding hands and singing and moving together?

The group moves to the ending ritual. The worker has helped the group solve the problem of missing a loved one. The worker emphasizes the good feeling of being together. Note that sexual feelings are dealt with openly. Everyone's sense of loss is expressed tieing the group together with a common feeling.

Termination
When a Worker Leaves the Group or a Group Member dies

Stage Two and Three people do not mourn death. They have come to terms with dying. When a group member dies, acknowledge the death and find a replacement using the recommendations of other staff members. Usually group members will not remember the person who is gone.

Stage Two and Three can end a relationship without being hurt. The worker is easily replaced, providing a new worker listens, touches and validates. It is those qualities that are remembered from week to week and not no much a matter of personalities. Disoriented old-old substitute people. A new worker will be quickly accepted. The departing worker should introduce the replacement at a farewell party to ease the transition. When I left my group that had been going for 10 years, the group members simply said: "Bye!" They easily transferred their trust to the person who took my place. Whenever you leave, always be honest. Tell the people when you are coming back, if you are coming back. Admit your own loss when you leave.

How Validation Groups Compare with other Groups[56] [57]

Unlike a group for oriented people, a Validation group is highly structured. The worker is directive, leading the group through the beginning, middle and end. Oriented members of groups assume roles spontaneously, sit where they want to, discuss topics that have not been selected by the worker, they choose the topics themselves. Oriented old-old are more verbal and don't regularly use music, touch or movement.

A Reminiscing group recalls memories from the past. Reminiscing usually begins with, "I remember when..." It requires a certain amount of attention span and enough verbal ability to express the memories, and an awareness of the difference between present and past time. Reminiscing is a Validation technique that is effective with maloriented elderly, who trust the worker, but not effective with time-confused or those in repetitive motion. Reminiscence therapy is different from reminiscing. One of the goals of Reminiscence therapy is to provide insight into past patterns of behavior in order to change present patterns of behavior. This is something that Stage Two and Three people are not capable of, nor are they helped by structured analysis. A maloriented person could go into a Reminiscing group, but not into Reminiscence therapy because they do not want to have insight.

Reality Orientation is based on the belief that disoriented people benefit from knowing present day reality. An RO group meets generally once a day for 30 minutes and relies on the use of clocks and calendars. Participants are encouraged to read and write. While a maloriented person can benefit from this sort of group, if it is not patronizing, a time-confused person, or a person in repetitive motion will withdraw, become hostile, begin to wander or show other rejecting behavior. In Validation, awareness of reality is often a side effect, but not a goal.

A Remotivation group meets one or two times a week; discussion topics are objective, involving activities that people have experienced and remember. Feelings are not explored. Again, maloriented people can greatly benefit from such a group, however more disoriented residents don't have the necessary attention span, verbal ability or emotional control. They need to express their feelings, and factual topics are only springboards for them to dive into their personal realities.

Behavior modification stems from the belief that all behavior is learned in three ways: respondent conditioning, that is, when one stimulus becomes associated with another (Pavlov's classical learning theory); operant conditioning, that is, negative and positive reinforcement (Skinner's theory); and imitation, that is, watching and copying other's behavior. Behaviorists do not believe in the Validation idea that adult social norms do not apply to disoriented old-old people, that acting out feelings or scenes from the past are appropriate behavior. Behaviorists try to change and limit the "negative" behavior through negative and positive reinforcement, and diversion. I have found that this does not work. Disoriented old-old are not aware that they are being punished through negative reinforcement, will not remember the positive reinforcement and are only momentarily distracted by diversion. There will be no long term change because the basic, underlying reason for the behavior is not addressed. For example, an old man in Stage Three is pounding his fist on a table. A nurse gives him a cup of coffee and he stops pounding in order to drink the coffee. He will certainly begin pounding again because he is pounding the table to get "order in the court." He was a judge and misses his job, his role in life. He is trying to feel worthwhile and a cup of coffee does not fill this deep, basic human need.

Validation and psychotherapy share many beliefs such as:
- early learning affects behavior throughout a lifetime.
- people have to want to change, they can not be forced to change.
- permanent change happens after there is insight.
- people feel better when they have expressed their emotions to a trusted listener.

They also share the following goals:
- to increase self-esteem.
- to increase feelings of well-being.
- to help a person cope with stress.

The key difference in these two therapies is the concept of achieving insight. Maloriented persons do not want to be confronted with their denials and confabulations; they will withdraw or become hostile. A time-confused person or person in repetitive motion does not have the cognitive ability to achieve insight.

Implementing Validation on an Institutional Level

Step 1: Introduce Validation to staff in all departments

- Give a brief overview of the history, the principals and the goals of Validation. Define the population that does and does not benefit from Validation.
- Show a video or film suggested at the back of this book, that clearly demonstrates what Validation is and how it works.
- At the end of the meeting pass around a sign up sheet for people who want to know more about Validation and want to join your Validation team.
- At a later stage, you will want to have Validation included on a policy level, as part of the interdisciplinary care plan.

Step 2: Form a Validation team

- If possible include some members from all levels of staff, housekeeping, dietary, administration, maintenance, nursing, social service, recreational therapies, occupational and physical therapy, etc.
- Plan to meet with your team weekly. At first you need to inform them about Validation. They need to learn the stages of disorientation and the appropriate Validation techniques for each stage. Use the *Individual Validation Treatment Plan* (page 110) and have each team member select an individual with whom they would like to work on an individual basis. Help them to

complete the form.

- Each week you need to share your experiences and evaluate your progress. The *Evaluation of Progress Form* (page 114) will help. During these team meeting you can release feelings about resident that you have not expressed.
- Other staff members will learn by watching you and your team practice Validation and seeing your results.
- After having worked for at least three months with Individual Validation, you can begin planning your Validation group.

Step 3: Begin a Validation group

If possible, have a co-worker, who can take over whenever necessary. The role of worker and co-worker are interchangeable, but it is important that at each group meeting, there is only one main worker. The co-worker's role is that of support. He or she should:

- help with the movement section of the program;
- assist in bringing people to and from the meeting;
- sit next to the person in repetitive motion;
- take people out of the group if they become disruptive;
- help evaluate progress after the meeting and choose a topic for the next meeting.

The worker and co-worker should support each other on an emotional level as well.

Follow the procedures for beginning a group as outlined earlier in Part Four.

Step 4: Begin a Family group

Three or four times a year, invite family members to an information session about Validation. Keep them informed of their relative's progress in both individual and group Validation. If they are interested, teach the family members specific techniques that will help them communicate more effectively, and improve their relationship with their relative. They will be motivated to visit more often.

Step 5: Review Validation progress with the entire staff every six months.

CHARTS, FORMS, TESTS

Differences in Behavior between Late Onset and Early Onset
Demented Populations

Assessing Observable Behaviors

The Stage Beyond Integrity: Feil's Resolution versus Vegetation
Stage

Individual Validation Treatment Plan

History and Baseline Behavior

Selecting Members for Validation Groups

Evaluation of Progress Form

Validation Group Summary Form

Evaluating Your Validation Skills

Validation Homework Assignments

Differences in Behavior between Late Onset and Early Onset Demented Populations

EARLY ONSET (45-75 years)

- Seldom live more than 85 years.
- Most have a home, family, social role or position.
- Do not want to withdraw from present reality.
- Purposeless, robot-like movements.
- Sight, hearing, mobility intact.
- Eyes remain blank, unfocused when validated or touched.
- Usually will not restore social roles in a Validation group.
- Usually cannot control behavior.
- Validation worker cannot establish goals for individual's progress.
- Frustrated in early stages of Alzheimer's, when aware of cognitive losses.
- Progressive deterioration until death, regardless of Validation.
- Hit out without provocation.
- Often do not respond to Validation when angry.
- Often cannot swallow.
- Often have seizures in the last stages.
- Deteriorate to vegetation regardless of Validation.

LATE ONSET (75+ years)

- Live a long time according to human longevity. (90+)
- Have lost their home, spouse, social role.
- Choose (on a subliminal level) to deny painful losses.
- Return to the past for comfort and to resolve unfinished issues.
- Graceful, rhythmical movements.
- Deterioration of sight, hearing and mobility.
- Respond with increased orientation to Validation.
- Speech often improves and eyes light when validated.
- Adult controls return when validated.
- Usually unaware of increasing cognitive losses.
- Validation worker can establish clear individual goals.
- Deterioration lessens when validated. (Unless individual suffers a stroke or great physical trauma)
- Will control anger when validated; rarely hit out without provocation.
- Express wisdom.
- Express basic human needs through non-verbal behaviors.
- Often help early onset demented residents, and help each other in a Validation group.

Assessing Observable Behavior

	CONTROL OF BODY-FUNCTIONS AND FEELINGS	EYE AND BODY MOVEMENT	RESPONSE TO LOSSES
Age 80+, oriented, but has physical problem.	Wants to feed, dress, and toilet self. Accepts help. Controls feelings appropriately.	Eyes focused, direct, bright. Muscles relaxed, unless paralyzed. Steady, even, sustained gait. Direct movement in wheelchair or walker. Wants to increase range of motion. Aware of loss of control.	Grieves appropriately. Aphasic expresses loss non-verbally. Moves on to new object-relationships, after death of loved ones, loss of job or body-part.
Age 80+, mentally ill.	Can feed, dress, and toilet self. Is unpredictable. Demands or refuses help. Keeps tight control or acts out feelings openly. Can control, if motivated.	Eyes darting or staring. Jaw tight. Face muscles tight. Erratic gait. Stiff movements. Darts in space. Often bent forward when moving.	Cannot expose intimate feelings to a trusted "other." Does not trust. Blames others or self for evil-doing.
Age 45-80, Alzheimer's disease. (Formerly pre-senile dementia, seldom lives to 80+).	Overdresses, underdresses; gradually loses ability to dress, toilet, feed. Becomes unaware of angry or sad feelings. Loss is progressive. Cannot understand changes in feelings or intellect. Often has seizures, loses ability to swallow.	Eyes unfocused, blank. Cannot bring finger to tip of nose. Mechanical, robot-like gait. Jerky, awkward movement in space. Purposeless, non-directive walk. Does not move towards an object or person. Uncoordinated.	Aware of loss to thinking centers in early stages. Is not aware of losses in later stages. Denies feelings, possibly due to lack of awareness.

103

Age 80+, Stage One, Malorientation, occasional confusion.	Can feed, dress, and toilet self. Wants to hold onto controls and capacities. Confabulates (pretends). Controls feelings rigidly. Seldom expresses feelings.	Eyes focused, direct. Purposeful, rigid, precise movements in space. Precise control of personal belongings. Often stores or hoards to keep control. Fingers pointed, arms folded. Protects self. Keeps self together. Muscles tight.	Denies grief. Denies losses due to aging. Holds onto outworn roles from the past. Denies memory loss. Returns to past conflicts to solve them.
Age 80+, Stage Two, Time Confusion. Stage Three, Repetitive Motion.	Stage Two needs help in dressing. Can often toilet and feed self. Stage Three needs help in all daily living functions. Does not wish to control feelings. Both express feelings freely, to resolve old issues from the past.	Stage Two: eyes waver, looking for the past. Rhythmic, free, loose movements in space. Dances with grace. Sits upright in chair. Stage Three: bangs, pats, paces, pounds, rocks in even rhythms. Moves loosely in space. Repeats movements. Eyes often closed. Hands clasped or folded. Loses awareness of body in space through sensory damage. Both have loose facial muscles.	Stage Two and Three no longer deny feelings. They express grief, anger, etc. freely. They retreat to the past to survive deep feelings of loss. They panic when aware of losses. They blot out painful reality by re-creating images from the past.

Assessing Observable Behavior

	RESPONSE TO RULES AND SOCIAL NORMS	RESPONSE TO TIME, PLACE, PERSON
Age 80+, Oriented, but with physical problem.	Accepts social norms. Accepts physical and social limitations. Compromises when wishes cannot be fulfilled. Seeks substitute pleasures. Sublimates sexual and hostile feelings in socially approved channels. Wants approval.	Is aware of clock time. Accepts recent memory loss. Finds ways to keep track of appointments, names, etc. Classifies people and objects appropriately. Compares similar and different objects, using metaphoric speech. Reviews the past. Aphasic re-trains cognitive functions to classify objects.
Age 80+, mentally ill	Has rejected rules throughout life. Has often been hospitalized. Cannot hold a job. No intimate "gut-level" friends. Delusions, images, and hallucinations based on fabricated people & objects, not on loved ones from the past.	Names and classifies correctly. Knows clock time. Feels others hurt them. Fabricates people and objects. Fears are not related to aging, they have been going on for a lifetime.
Age 45-80, Alzheimer's disease. (Formerly, pre-senile dementia. Seldom lives to 80+).	Tries to hold onto rules and social skills in early stages. Conforms in early stages. Wants to dress well. Performs in a ritualistic, mechanical way. In last stage, can no longer perform. Is unaware of rules. Has no insight into loss of social skills.	Loses track of time, place and person. Is aware of losses in early stages. Loses track of names and roles of loved ones. In unaware of losses in later stage. Loses ability to use and name objects. Loses recognition and cognition.

Age 80+, Stage One, Malorientation	Holds onto rules. Keeps track of social obligations. Is threatened by those who do not follow rules. Wants things in place according to specifications. Wants approval of authority. Hoards.	Is aware of present time, place and person. Is frightened by occasional recent memory loss. Wants to think clearly. Uses humor to cover losses. Wants to justify the past; to sum up life.
Age 80+, Stage Two, Time Confusion Stage Three, Repetitive Motion	No longer wants to conform to social rules. Retreats. Blots out present authority's rules. Does not want approval of present caregivers. Wants approval of past loved ones and turns to significant others from the past for rules of behavior. Restores early childhood rules. Will not modify behavior unless motivated.	Does not use clock time. Measures time by memories. "Sees" people and places from the past in vivid images. Replaces damage to sight, hearing and movement with "inner-sight", "inner-hearing", and memories of moving in the past. Relives and restores the past to resolve living and regain identity.

Assessing Observable Behavior

	VERBAL COMMUNICATION	NON-VERBAL COMMUNICATION, USE OF SYMBOLS	APPROPRIATE GROUP
Age 80+, oriented with physical problem.	Communicates to gain understanding. Uses humor. Verbally ties past with present to gain integrity. Wants to be understood.	Aphasic uses eye contact and gestures to communicate. Low, even relaxed voice-tone. Keeps personal distance, unless intimate with family. Can read and write, although is often shaky.	Task-oriented, such as: baking, art, music, pottery, writing, humor group ("Aha," brings a belly laugh, "Ha ha," restores well-being.)
Age 80+, mentally ill	Seldom listens. Answers according to mood. Names people and objects correctly. Rambles or is silent. Speaks in harsh, whiny tones.	Avoids direct eye contact. Avoids touch. Acts out instinctive needs. Little metaphoric thinking. Switches people and objects.	Remotivation groups with objective stimuli; Reality orientation that is not patronizing. Caring workers help mentally ill people.
Age 45-80 Alzheimer's disease, (Formerly, pre-senile dementia, seldom lives to 80+)	Speech is garbled. Cannot classify objects. Forgets names. Does not connect thoughts. Cannot make choices.	Does not recall touch. Uses hand gestures. Random movements. Cannot read or write.	A Validation group can stimulate interaction. Trips to familiar spots can stimulate dormant speech and well-being in early stages.

Age 80+, Stage One: Maloriented	Wants verbal reminder of time and place. Uses dictionary words, complex sentences, humor, sarcasm, repeats same stories. Seeks facts to understand.	Controls eye-contact. Avoids touch. Keeps personal distance. Uses symbols to express old conflicts (see pages 47-49) Reads and writes.	A political discussion group gives an outlet for hostility. A task oriented group, non-patronizing Reality Orientation group and Remotivation group help maintain well-being.
Age 80+, Stage Two: Time Confusion Stage Three: Repetitive Motion	Blends sounds, to form unique, personal words. There is little use of dictionary words. Returns to early emotionally tinged words and sounds, rhymes. Restores the past through forming sounds. Cannot use logical, as-if reasoning. Cannot use metaphors.	Body parts, objects and people in present time, become people and familiar objects from the past. Feelings are freely expressed. Communication is largely non-verbal. Often reads, but cannot write.	Validation groups acknowledge feelings, respect the need of old-old people to restore the past when the present has lost meaning. Well established social roles return. Stress lessens. Gait improves. Dormant speech can return, social interactions produce well being. They will not vegetate.

The Stage Beyond Integrity: Feil's Resolution versus Vegetation Stage

	STAGE ONE: MALORIENTATION	STAGE TWO: TIME CONFUSION	STAGE THREE: REPETITIVE MOTION	STAGE FOUR: VEGETATION
BASIC HELPING CUES FOR THE CARE-GIVER	- use who, what, where, when and how questions - use minimal touch - maintain social distance	- use preferred sense - use touch and eye contact - use ambiguous pronouns - match their emotions	- use touch, eye contact - mirror emotions and movements	- mirror movements - use sensory stimulation - use music
ORIENTATION	- keep track of time - hold onto present reality - realize and are threatened by own disorientation	- do not keep track of clock time - forget facts, names, places	- shut out most stimuli from outside world - have own sense of time	- do not recognize family, visitors, old friends or staff - no time sense
BODY PATTERNS: muscles	- tense, tight muscles - usually continent - quick, direct movements - purposeful gait	- sit upright but relaxed - aware of incontinence - slow, smooth movements - dance-like gait	- slumped forward - unaware of incontinence - restless, pacing - repeats early childhood movements and sounds	- placid, slump - little movement, fetal position - no effort to control continence - frequent finger movements
vocal tone	- harsh, accusatory, and often whining - can sing	- low, rarely harsh - sing and laugh readily	- melodic - slow and steady tone	
eyes	- focused, good eye contact	- clear, unfocused - downcast, eye contact triggers recognition	- eyes usually closed	- eyes shut (face lacks expression)

EMOTIONS	- deny feelings	- substitute memories and feelings from past, to present situations	- demonstrate feelings openly	- difficult to assess
PERSONAL CARE	- can do basic care	- misplace personal items - need help with basic care	- cannot care for themselves	- cannot care for themselves
COMMUNICATION	- communicate clearly - use dictionery words	- begin to use uniques word combinations - have difficulty with nouns	- communicate mainly on a non verbal level - substitute movement for speech	- difficult to assess
MEMORY AND SOCIAL BEHAVIOR	- some short-term memory loss, which they find disturbing - can read and write - conform to rules and conventions	- have "selective" memory, mainly long-term - can read, but no longer write legibly - create up own rules	- early memories and universal symbols are the most meaningful - cannot read or write - have no rules	- difficult to assess
HUMOR	- retain some humor	- can not play games with rules (Bingo, etc.) - unique humor	- laugh easily, often unprompted	- difficult to assess

Individual Validation Treatment Plan

Date: Validation Worker:

Resident's Name:_____

Stage of disorientation:
Maloriented Time Confused Repetitive Motion Vegetation
(notes)_____

Contact Time: _____ minutes per day, ___ days per weeks

VERBAL VALIDATION:
Topics to discuss:_____

Unfinished life task:_____

Preferred sense:_____

Validation techniques:_____

NON-VERBAL VALIDATION:
Task-oriented movements: (baking, folding, mixing, etc.)
_____

Repetitive movements to match and mirror:
_____

Song titles to sing:_____

_____

Appropriate touch:_____

Validation techniques:_____

_____

Sit resident next to: _____

Encourage them to (sing, talk about, move, touch, etc.): _____

_____

Equipment needed: (Validation apron, bean bag, ball, pots to wash, etc.) _____

_____

Individual Validation Treatment Plan: Column Two
VALIDATION TECHNIQUES:

Use the techniques that are appropriate for the stage of disorientation. (See Part Three) Remember, a person can change from stage to stage within a short period of time.

• Observe their physical characteristics.

• Listen to the words the person uses.

• Match their preferred sense.*

• Ask: who, what, where, when, how. (avoid why.)

• Repeat their key words, paraphrase, summarize.

• Ask the extreme. (How bad? Worse? Best? etc.)

• Reminisce. (How did it used to be before...?)

• Imagine the opposite. (When were things better? Is there a time when ... doesn't happen?)

• Can we find a creative solution together? What did you do when this happened before? Tap an earlier coping method that worked.

• Center yourself. Put your own feelings in the closet.

• Observe their gut emotion.

• Say the emotion out loud, with emotion. Match the emotion.

• Mirror their movement. Pick up their breathing. Match rhythms.

• Link their behavior with the unmet need: love, safety, to be useful, to express gut emotions, to be listened to.

• Touch: (their cheek, back of the head, jaw, shoulder, upper arm, etc.)

• Maintain genuine eye contact.

• Use ambiguity, a vague pronoun, (he, it, someone, that, etc.) when you cannot understand the word doodles.

• Sing familiar songs that match their feelings.

* Preferred sense words:
Visual: look, picture, see, notice, watch, clear, bright, etc.
Hearing: sounds like, loud, scratchy, noisy, clear, still, etc.
Feeling: hits, strikes, hurts, scary, touches, hard, heavy, etc.

HISTORY AND BASELINE BEHAVIOR

Resident's Name _____

Precautions _____

Personal Information: age, sex, race, birthplace, employment history, children, etc.	Family background, socio-economic and religious background, close family relationships (names).
Health Information: medical diagnosis, length of hospitalizations, medications, physical losses.	In This Home: Friends? Activities? Movement? Relationship to staff? Night-time behavior vs. day time. Eating behavior.
Action Patterns: Customary response to crisis, losses. What precipitated hospitalization? What is the preferred sense? Typical relationships. Physical behavior: muscles, movement in space, eye contact, response to touch.	Typical emotional patterns. Expresses feelings? Denies feelings? Which feelings are most often expressed? (anger, love, fear, grief)
Stage of Disorientation: malorientation? time-confusion? repetitive motion? vegetation? Psychotic behavior? Fluctuates between stages?	Recommended Validation treatment: Individual? Group? Give details. What role? Where should they sit?

Selecting Members for Validation Groups

Questions for staff and family members. "Yes" answers indicate a Stage One level of disorientation. Seven or more "yes" answers indicate a life time of mental illness. Do not include either in a Validation group.

1. Has the person ever been admitted to a mental hospital?
2. Does this person blame others for physical losses?
3. Does this person blame others for social losses?
4. Does this person know where he/she lives?
5. Does the person know where he/she lived before? The names of his/her children? The names of staff members?
6. Does this person have a history of retardation?
7. Does the person remember an intimate relationship with someone he/she loved, but blames this person for his/her losses?
8. Has the person been unable to form an intimate relationship?
9. Does the person hold onto rules rigidly?
10. Is the person wary of expressing feelings?

Seven or more "yes" answers to the following questions indicate aphasia or organic diseases that do NOT accompany normal aging. Do not include this person in a Validation group.

1. The person uses correct speech, omitting small connecting words, such as "and, but, I, they, up, down," etc.
2. Cries when happy, laughs when sad.
3. Swears constantly.
4. Is rigid in body movement, mechanical (without drugs.)
5. Dresses well, is socially correct, but NOT oriented to present time.
6. Understands what is said, but cannot express him or herself.
7. Has a sense of humor.
8. Can read a newspaper.
10. Can play bingo, or games with rules.
11. Does not make eye contact or respond to nurturing touch.
12. Does not respond to caring voice tone.

Questions to ask residents. Repeated references to the past indicate Stage Two or Three disorientation.

1. Who do you miss most? Your spouse? Your children?
2. What did you do to earn a living?
3. Did you mind leaving your home to move here?
4. What is the worst thing about getting old?
5. How do you overcome sadness?
6. What is the most important thing in life?
7. What happened to you that brought you here?
8. Do you have a lot of pain? (Stage Two and Three do not complain of pain as often as more oriented residents.)
9. Were you in a hospital? What did the doctors do?
10. Do you like the other people here? If not, why?
11. Do you like the staff? Who don't you like? (Stage Two and Three will say they live at "home" and do not recognize staff.)

114

EVALUATION OF PROGRESS FORM

Fill out this form after each group or individual meeting. Rate each person as follows:
0 - never; 1 - rarely; 2 - occasionally; 3 - frequently; 4 - always.

Date	Name	Stage	Talks	Makes eye contact	Touches	Smiles	Takes Leadership role in group	Participates (physically): dances, sings.	Other, personal behavior. Comments and notes for the next meeting.

VALIDATION GROUP SUMMARY

Date: _____   Name of Group: _____

Validation worker: _____

INVITATION TO GROUP MEETING TODAY: (list unusual responses)

MAIN ISSUES AND EVENTS:

PLANS FOR NEXT MEETING:

COMMENTS AND RECOMMENDATIONS:

VALIDATION GROUP SUMMARY
                        SAMPLE

Date: 3/8/91   Name of Group: The Tuesday Group

Validation worker: N. Feil

INVITATION TO GROUP MEETING TODAY: (list unusual responses)

Mrs. Smith refused to come. She looks very sick
Mr. Stout kissed me.

MAIN ISSUES AND EVENTS:

Discussion of sexual needs, missing husbands and wives. Mr. Stout misses his wife. He
will become either the Host or Head Dancer to fill his needs to be with women.

PLANS FOR NEXT MEETING:

Topic: death of a parent.
Songs: "Jesus Loves Me", "I want a Girl", "Rock a Bye Baby"
Problem to solve: When you're lonely and miss your parents, what can you do?
        Ask Mrs. Tubin if she prays or looks for friends.
        Other solutions: sing a lullaby, take a walk, read a poem, remember your mother
Movement: rocking to music holding a big elastic band.
Refreshments: coffee and cookies

COMMENTS AND RECOMMENDATIONS:

Find out from the head nurse if Mrs. Smith has heart trouble.
Let Mr. Stout sit next to Mrs. Cone. Encourage them to dance.
Get "Let Me Call You Sweetheart" record.
Next meeting, celebrate Mrs. Smith's 90th birthday. Topic: getting older.

The following tests can be given to evaluate potential Validation workers (people who will be working with Alzheimer's type populations) in an institution or organization.

Circle the correct answer.

1. A disoriented resident screams every time she drops her purse. Should you:
   (a) Try to make sure she has the purse. Explore to build trust. Find out what the purse means to her.
   (b) Assure her that she has no need for the purse in this place. She isn't going anywhere. She doesn't need money.
   (c) Take her purse away. "Out of sight out of mind."

2. A disoriented old-old man unzips his pants in public. Should you:
   (a) Gently walk with him to his room, and ask, "Do you miss your wife?"
   (b) Negatively reinforce him. Firmly let him know, "We don't do things like that around here."
   (c) Mirror his actions.

3. A disoriented resident hollers, "I want my teeth!" Should you:
   (a) Find out where her teeth are, or get her false teeth if needed.
   (b) Tell her that she always takes her teeth out and loses them.
   (c) Tell her she is too old for new dentures.

4. When you are with a disoriented person, are you most inclined to:
   (a) Keep your distance.
   (b) Touch them softly to elicit interaction.
   (c) Stand close without touching.
   (d) Use soft touch together with close eye contact.

5. When a person is in Stage Three (repetitive motion), I:
   (a) Mirror their actions using touch and close eye contact.
   (b) Ask them what they are doing.
   (c) Ask them to stop.
   (d) Ignore their actions.

Please mark either (T) True, or (F) False.

6. ( ) Almost all old-old people who are disoriented are incontinent.

7. ( ) All old people ought to know their married name, where they are, the present date and time.

8. ( ) People who live in the past are happy that way, so it's better to pretend to believe them.

9. ( ) People who are over 80 years old and disoriented, with physical failures and social losses, turn to the past to resolve old conflicts and to restore old pleasures.

10.( ) It is important to correct disoriented people when they are mistaken or forgetful.

11.( ) It is important for older people to have alternative interests to prevent withdrawal.

Please answer the following in essay form. Use additional paper.

12. List Erikson's six life stages and their related tasks.

13. Identify and describe the four stages of disorientation.

14. Describe the goals and needs of old-old people in each of the four stages.

15. Describe the Validation techniques that are useful for each stage of disorientation.

16. List the steps involved in centering yourself.

17. List the steps necessary in forming a Validation group (for the first time).

18. Write a brief introduction of Validation, as you might present it to family members or staff.

Answers to questions 1-11 are on page 121

VALIDATION HOMEWORK ASSIGNMENTS

The following forms can be used to help train co-workers or family members in the use of Validation techniques.

Assignment 1: Discover the preferred sense of the following persons and justify your "diagnosis" by stating clues that tipped you off.

A) Your partner (or other intimate person):
Preferred sense: _____

    Clues: _____

    _____

B) Your child:
Preferred sense: _____

    Clues: _____

    _____

C) A Co-worker:
Preferred sense: _____

    Clues: _____

D) A resident:
Preferred sense: _____

    Clues: _____

E) Resident #2:
Preferred sense: _____

    Clues: _____

Assignment 2: List as many words as you can which can serve as responses when talking with a person identified as having the following preferred sense.

HEARING   SEEING   FEELING

_____   _____   _____
_____   _____   _____
_____   _____   _____
_____   _____   _____
_____   _____   _____
_____   _____   _____
_____   _____   _____
_____   _____   _____
_____   _____   _____
_____   _____   _____
_____   _____   _____
_____   _____   _____
_____   _____   _____
_____   _____   _____
_____   _____   _____
_____   _____   _____
_____   _____   _____
_____   _____   _____
_____   _____   _____
_____   _____   _____
_____   _____   _____
_____   _____   _____
_____   _____   _____
_____   _____   _____
_____   _____   _____
_____   _____   _____

These assignments were created by Mary Bayer, R.N.
Sandy River Alliance Nursing Care Centers in Portland, Maine

Answers to the *Evaluating Your Validation Skills* Quiz

Question	Answer
1	a
2	a
3	a
4	d
5	a
6	T
7	F
8	F
9	T
10	F
11	T

FOOTNOTES

1. Naomi Feil, "Group Therapy in a Home for the Aged," *The Gerontologist* 7, No.3, Part I (September 1967): 192-195.

2. Edward Feil, *The Tuesday Group*, film (Cleveland, Ohio: Edward Feil Productions, 1972).

3. "History of Isadore Rose." Unpublished Case History, Montefiore Home, Cleveland, Ohio, 1963-71, available from Author.

4. Naomi Feil, "A New Approach to Group Therapy." Unpublished paper presented at the 25th Annual Meeting of the Gerontological Society in San Juan, Puerto Rico, December, 1972.

5. Erik Erikson, *Insight and Responsibility* (New York: W.W.Norton & Co., 1964).

6. Erik Erikson, *Childhood and Society* (New York: W.W.Norton & Co., 1950, 1963).

7. Erik H. and Joan M. Erikson, "Introduction: Reflections On Aging," in 'Stuart Spicker, Kathleen Woodward and David Van Tassel (eds), *Aging And The Elderly* (Atlantic Highlands, N.J.: Humanities Press, 1978).

8. Gail Sheehy, *Passages* (New York: E.P.Dutton & Co., 1974).

9. Sue V. Saxon and Mary Jean Etten, *Physical Change and Aging* (New York: Tiresias Press, 1978).

10. James J. Barrell and Donald D. Price, "Two Experimental Orientations Toward a Stressful Situation and Their Somatic and Visceral Responses", *Psychophysiology* 14 (1977): 517-521.

11. F.G. Schettler and G.S. Boyd, *Atherosclerosis* (Amsterdam, the Netherlands: North-Holland Publishing Co./Biomedical Press, 1969).

12. Wilder Penfield, "The Cerebral Cortex and the Mind of Man," in: Peter Laslett (ed.), *The Physical Basis of Mind* (New York: Macmillan Co., 1950).

13. N. Feil and J. Flynn, "Meaning Behind Movements of the Disoriented Old-Old," *Somatics* IV, No.2 (Spring/Summer 1983).

14. Willard Mittelman, "Self-Actualization," *Journal of Humanistic Psychology* 31 (Winter 1991): 114-135.

15. A. Zaidel, "The Concept of Cerebral Dominance in the Split Brain," in: E.W. Busse (ed.), *Cerebral Correlates of Conscious Experience* (Amsterdam, the Netherlands: North-Holland Publishing Co.): 263-284.

16. P. Watzlawick, J. Bevin and D.D. Jackson, *Pragmatics of Human Communication* (New York: W.W. Norton & Co., 1967).

17. See Note 12.

18. Russell Brain, "Speech and Thought," and Wilder Penfield, "The Cerebral Cortex and the Mind of Man", in: Peter Laslett, op. cit.

19. Jean Piaget, *The Origins of Intelligence in Children* (New York: W.W. Norton & Co., 1952).

20. Edward Feil, *Looking for Yesterday*, film (Cleveland, Ohio: Edward Feil Productions, 1978).

21. J.B. Aker, Arthur C. Walsh and J.R. Beam, *Mental Capacity, Medical and Legal Aspects of Aging* (New York: McGraw-Hill Book Co., 1977).

22. Adrian Verwoerdt, *Clinical Geropsychiatry* (Baltimore, Md.: Williams & Wilkins Co., 1976).

23. Julius Weil, "Special Program for the Senile in Home for the Aged," *Geriatrics* 21 (January 1966): 197-202.

24. R.N. Butler and Myrna I. Lewis, *Aging and Mental Health* (New York: C.V. Mosby Co., 1977): 76-83.

25. Marian Emr, "Progress Report on Senile Dementia of the Alzheimer's Type." *NIH Publication*, No. 81-2342 (Rockville, Md.: National Institute on Aging, September 1981).

26. R.N. Butler and Myrna I. Lewis, op. cit., p.88.

27. G. Blessed, B.E. Tomlinson and M. Roth, "The Association between Quantitative Measures of Dementia and of Senile Change in the Cerebral Grey Matter of Elderly Subjects," *British Journal of Psychiatry* 114 (1968): 797-811.

28. Leonard L. Heston and June A. White, *The Vanishing Mind* (New York: W.H. Freeman & Co., 1983, 1991).

29. Dennis J. Selkoe, "Amyloid Protein and Alzheimer's Disease," *Scientific American*, November 1991.

30. See Note 22.

31. Thomas Harris, *I'm OK, You're OK* (New York: Harper & Row, 1967).

32. Beth Rubin, "Burnout; Causation And Measurement." Unpublished Master's Thesis, Department of Psychology, Michigan State University, East Lansing, Michigan, 1982.

33. Naomi Feil, "Group Work with Disoriented Nursing Home Residents," *Social Work with Groups* 5, No.2 (New York: Haworth Press, Summer 1982): 57.

34. See Note 4.

35. Naomi Feil, "A Comparison of Oriented and Disoriented Residents." Unpublished study, Montefiore Home, Cleveland, Ohio, 1976.

36. Stan Alprin, "The Study to Determine the Results of Implementing Validation Therapy." Unpublished study, Cleveland State University, September 1980.

37. Marlene Peoples, "Validation Therapy Versus Reality Orientation As Treatment for Disoriented Institutionalized Elderly." Unpublished Master's Thesis, College of Nursing, University of Akron, Akron, Ohio, 1982.

38. Paul Fritz, "The Language of Resolution Among The Old-Old: The Effect of Validation Therapy on Two Levels of Cognitive Confusion." Research results presented to the Speech Communication Association, November 1986, Chicago, Illinois.

39. James T. Dietch, Linda J. Hewett and Sue Jones, "Adverse Effects of Reality Orientation, *Journal of American Geriatric Society* 37 (1989): 974-976.

40. Colin Sharp and Alan Johns, "Validation Therapy: an Evaluation of a Program at the South Port Community Nursing Home in Melbourne, Australia." Paper presented at the Australian Association of Voluntary Care Associations, Melbourne, Victoria, Australia, November 10-13, 1991.

41. Ian Morton and Christine Bleathman, "Does It Matter Whether It's Tuesday or Friday?" *Nursing Times* 84, No. 6 (London, 1988), 25-27.

42. Jean Prentczynski, Thesis, Department of Medicine, University of Reims, France, December 20 1991.

43. Gay Hendriks and Russel Wills, *The Centering Book* (Englewood Cliffs, N.J.: Prentice-Hall, 1975).

44. Sigmund Freud, *The Basic Writings of Sigmund Freud*, vol I: *The Psychopathology of Everyday Life* (New York: Random House, 1938): 35-150.

45. Jolande Jacobi, *Complex/Archetype/Symbol in the Psychology of C.G.Jung* (Princeton: Princeton/Bollington Edition, 1971).

46. See Note 45.

47. R. Bandler, J. Grinder and V. Satir, *Changing With Families* (Palo Alto, Cal.: Science and Behavior Books, 1976).

48. M. L. von Franz and J. Hillman, *Jung's Typology* (Zürich: Spring Publications, 1975).

49. See Note 49.

50. P.K. Saha in: Edward Feil, *The More We Get Together*, film (Cleveland, Ohio: Edward Feil Productions, 1988).

51. See Note 13.

52. Adelaide Bry, *Visualization* (New York: Barnes and Noble Books, 1979).

53. R. Bandler and J. Grinder, *Frogs into Princes* (Salt Lake City, Utah: Real People Press, 1979).

54. Edward Feil, *Mrs. Ward*, film (Cleveland, Ohio: Edward Feil Productions, 1980).

55. Margaret E. Hartford, *Groups and Social Work* (New York and London: Columbia University Press, 1971).

56. Paul K. H. Kim (ed.), *Serving the Elderly* (New York: Eldine de Gruyter, 1991).

57. Gemma M.M. Jones and Bère M.L. Miesen (eds.), *Caregiving in Dementia* (London: Routledge, 1992).

ADDITIONAL BIBLIOGRAPHY

American Psychiatric Association, *Diagnostics and Statistical Manual of Mental Disorders II, III and IIIR* (Washington DC: American Psychiatric Association, 1952, 1980)
Robert N. Butler and Alexander G. Bearn (eds.), *The Aging Process, Therapeutic Implications* (New York: Raven Press, 1985).
Naomi Feil, "Resolution: The Final Life Task," *Journal of Humanistic Psychology* 25, No. 2 (Spring 1985): 91-105.
Naomi Feil, "Validation: An Empathic Approach to the Care of Dementia," *Clinical Gerontologist* 8, No. 3 (1989).
Howard Gardner, *The Shattered Mind* (New York: International Universities Press, 1949).
Herbert Ginsburg and Sylvia Opper, *Piaget's Theory of Intellectual Development* (Englewood Cliffs, N.J.: Prentice-Hall, 1969).
R. Gordon, *Your Healing Hands: The Polarity Experience* (Santa Cruz, Cal.: Unity Press, 1978).
Charles Hampden-Turner, *Maps of the Mind* (New York: Macmillan Co., 1981).
R.D. Laing, *The Divided Self* (Baltimore: Penguin Books, 1969).
Robert E. Ornstein, *The Psychology of Consciousness* (New York: Harcourt, Brace, Jovanovich, 1977).
Karl H. Pribham, *Languages of the Brain* (Monterey, Cal.: Wadsworth Publishing Co., 1977).
Carl Rogers, *Counseling and Psychotherapy* (Boston: Houghton Mifflin Co., 1942).
Carl Rogers, *Way of Being* (Boston: Houghton Mifflin Co., 1981).
Charles Wells, *Dementia* (Philadelphia, Pa.: F.A. Davis Co., 1977).
J. Welwood, "Befriending Emotion," *The Journal of Transpersonal Psychology* II, No. 2 (1979): 145.
Zepelin, Wolfe and Kleinplatz, "Evaluation of a Yearlong Reality Orientation Program," *The Journal of Gerontology* 36, No. 1 (January 1981): 70-77.

Edward Feil Productions Films and Videos:

Where Life Still Means Living, Montefiore Home, 1964 (24 min F&V).
The Inner World of Aphasia, Montefiore Home, 1968 (24 min. F&V).
The Tuesday Group, Montefiore Home, 1972 (14 min. F&V).
When Generations Meet, Montefiore Home, 1973 (24 min. F&V).
A New Life for Rose, C. Schnurmann Housing, 1973 (24 min. F&V).
Living the Second Time Around, 1974 (22 min. F&V).
Looking for Yesterday, Cleveland, 1978 (29 min. F&V).
100 Years To Live, Cleveland, 1981 (29 min. F&V).
My First Hundred Years, Cleveland, 1984 (57 min. V).
The More We Get Together, Cleveland, 1986 (44 min. V).
Act Your Age.- Marge the Blamer, Muriel the Wanderer, Cleveland, 1988 (21 min. V).
Communicating with the Alzheimer Type Population.: the Validation Method, Cleveland, 1988 (19 min. V).
Myrna: The Mal-Oriented, Cleveland, 1997 (26 min. V).
The Four Phases of Resolution, Cleveland, 1997 (8 min. V).
The Seminar Group, Cleveland, 1997 (8 min. V).

V=Video, F=Film

INDEX